DATE DUE

JUN 1 9 2005	
SEP 2 2 2005	
DEC 2 7 2007	

IMPROVISE THIS!

MARK BERGREN

MOLLY COX

JIM DETMAR

ILLUSTRATIONS BY R.O. BLECHMAN

IMPROVISE THIS!

HOW TO THINK ON YOUR FEET SO
YOU DON'T FALL ON YOUR FACE

HYPERION

NEW YORK

Library of Congress Cataloging-in-Publication Data

Bergren, Mark.
  Improvise this! : how to think on your feet without falling on your face /
Mark Bergren, Molly Cox, Jim Detmar.—1st ed.
      p.   cm.
  ISBN 0-7868-6774-4
  1. Customer services.   2. Selling.   I. Cox, Molly, 1959–   II. Detmar, Jim,
1956–   III. Title.

HF5415.5 .B465   2002
658.85—dc21

2001039999

FIRST EDITION

10   9   8   7   6   5   4   3   2   1

CONTENTS

Contents

ACKNOWLEDGMENTS

From all of us: Our heartfelt thanks to Sam Horn, who believed in this project from its conception, and to our agent, Laurie Liss, who truly "gets it." To Will Schwalbe and Mary Ellen O'Neill, our editors, thank you for your guidance and direction. To Kathy Hammer and Terry Joseph for your eagle editing eyes. Thanks goes to our assistant, Jen Scott, who worked at the office by day and improvised by night. And to the countless audience members who have attended our playshops and embraced the principles of improvisation.

Mark: I'd like to thank with all my heart the most wonderful family anyone could ever hope for—Patricia, Anne, and Claire. You keep me smiling. And love to my parents, Elaine and Carl, brother Paul and sisters Beth, Barbara, and Adele. I'm also grateful to all who've had the faith in me to say, "Yes!," especially Bill Coons, Dr. Jim McTeague, and Dudley Riggs. The same and more to all my friends and colleagues who've kept the faith in this crazed art of improvisation (and yes, it can be an *art*), including Paul Sills, the artists at the Brave New Workshop, the Comedy Warehouse, and at Disney, particularly my dear friends, Ken Kraft and Chris Oyen. Last but certainly not least, major league gratitude to my partners, pals, and confidants Jim and Molly, without whom our book and business would still just be a dream.

Molly: To Christina and Alex Ziton, I'm glad I'm your mother. Thank you for your smiles, love, and laughter. Bob, thank you for "comedy hour" and "tech support." Thanks to Julie Coe, Brenda Abdilla, and Amy Levey: my cheerleaders, and neurotic confidants. To Bill Dinon, Peggy Brask, Laura Ryan, Cate Lamkin, Linda Buckland, and Julie Lassig—my buddies. My siblings, Kathy, Anita, Chris, and Terry for providing me with endless comedic relief, and to Mom and Dad, thanks for your love, instilling me with confidence, and passing along the "author gene." Thanks to the Brave New Workshop, Stevie Rays, and the women of "Funny Women Fest." And finally to Jim and Mark who are my partners, my dear friends, and who make me laugh every single day.

Jim: The biggest joy of writing this book has been the people who have been there all along. Helping in ways they may never know. This includes my beautiful daughter Katie; Kelly—my inspiration; my siblings—Claudia, Scott, Mary Jo, Don; my Mom; Garry, Angela, and Alexander—you know why; my fostering family at the Comedy Warehouse; my hyperextended family at the Brave New Workshop; to every improviser who has shared the stage and their gifts with me; to Patricia, Claire, and Anne—I'll be in the basement; and finally Mark and Molly—I am so fortunate to have been blessed with two amazing friends and partners. This is truly just the end of the beginning.

INTRODUCTION
Curtain Up!

Consider this, if you will: You are onstage every day performing the scenes of your life in a play without a script. This book will help you tap into your natural abilities to take chances and calculated risks by learning how to improvise. Maybe you'll even end up more creative. In short, our goal is to help you to become more of who you are. This isn't about turning you into an improvisation actor or training you to conform to some corporate ideal. It's about giving you the confidence to be more flexible, spontaneous, and fun loving in your own authentic way, as you play these scenes of your life.

Each of us has countless opportunities to improvise. Perhaps you want to be more creative on demand in your job. Maybe you simply want to stop looking like a deer in the headlights when asked a question at your weekly manager meetings. Or an important personal opportunity knocks on your door but you freeze, on the advice of your old friend—indecision.

There are hundreds of scenarios like these where having the

ability to think on your feet and react with self-assurance would be an enormous asset.

In a combined thirty-five years of improvisation we've seen many fledgling improvisers take small steps, which lead to great leaps. We've seen incredible breakthroughs, unforeseen transformations, and monumental personal growth. (And okay, there was that one guy who sunk into the abyss of personal hell. But he would have anyway.)

Businesses are sending their top managers and frontline staff alike to improv classes in droves. Why? Because improv works! Improvisation theater techniques help you increase your confidence, spontaneity, and creativity.

And the interest in improvisation isn't just a fad. It's grounded in practical experience. It's been the best-kept secret of many a salesperson, CEO, and mother of five trying to survive. It's not just for the cast of *Whose Line Is It Anyway?* and *Second City* anymore. You can apply what's in this book at work and at home. If you're seeking an edge in a highly complicated, competitive world you need to be able to think on your feet!

In today's rough and tumble business culture, you're expected to keep up with the pace of changing technology as well as to outsmart your competition. In a larger sense, what really counts is your ability to adapt to frequent and sudden changes. Your willingness and ability to seize each change and embrace it with flexibility and spontaneity can mean the difference between mediocrity and success.

Also, some of the most important moments in our personal lives require assessing a situation with the same suppleness and quick thinking that is the basis of improvisation. More often than not, you're going to find yourself without a script.

So, we're asking you now to take a leap into improvisation— and we assure you the net will appear. Depending on whether or not you read our book, of course. See, this book could even save your life. Or it could make a fine coaster. It's all about how you see things.

Learning improvisation teaches you to pay attention. By putting yourself in a vulnerable position and experiencing new concepts and feelings, you'll discover things about yourself. You may be at a point where you just need a thorough dusting or a smidgen of WD-40. Improvisation helps you become unstuck. And yes, that's the technical term.

At the very least you'll develop a heightened sense of spontaneity when you step onto your life-stage each day. (Shower, put on your costume, and have a hearty breakfast first, please.) The result is you'll simply have more fun. And isn't that alone worth the price of the book? We can't promise you'll lose weight, become closer to God, or rekindle sparks in your marriage—but don't be surprised if it happens.

Simply Have More Fun

For example, take the title to this book—*Improvise This! How to Think on Your Feet So You Don't Fall on Your Face.* Here are some earlier titles we came up with together. And rejected. We brainstormed. We made ourselves laugh. We shocked our own sensibilities. (Which is a good thing.) We argued. We drank a lot of Starbucks. And as you'll see, we just simply had more fun.

A Few Choice Titles We Rejected

1. *Insights from the Top Improvisational Team Trainers: Sheer Genius or Neurological Disorder?*
2. *Murder, Maalox, and Mayhem for Managers*
3. *I'm OK—You're Fired!*

SO, WHAT IS IMPROV ANYWAY?

*Life is what happens to you while you're busy
making other plans.*

—John Lennon

Everyone improvises, every day. It's in our nature. It's what separates humans from robots, androids, microprocessors, and almost all candidates for public office. Life is indeed what happens while you're making other plans. And so is improvisation.

As much as we program our Palm Pilots or plot our next career move, life is unpredictable. And, since even the next moment of our life is unknown, we react to each new moment, relationship, or crisis in our day-to-day existence with an improvised response that is based on our experience, our habits, and our personality. Now we're not saying that each reaction is a good or even an appropriate improvised response. The captain of the *Titanic* brought all of his seafaring experience to bear, reacted "from the gut" (as good improvisers do) when he saw the iceberg, and made the wrong choice. However, he did improvise. And so do you—each time life throws you a curve and you face an unplanned situation with an equally unplanned, courageous, from-the-gut response. And we're certain that nine out of ten times, you've made the right choice and don't need to run panicked for the lifeboats, while the band plays on . . .

In recent years when the word "improvisation" or "improv" is bandied about, we often times visualize actors or comedians improvising on stage performing made-up, cheeky comedy scenes and songs based on suggestions from the audience— whether it's on Drew Carey's *Whose Line Is It Anyway?* or on the stage of countless Improv troupes scattered across the urban fun-scape of every city and on almost every college campus.

When this freewheeling spontaneity is done well (which is not always), when it is playful, funny, witty, surprising, sometimes touching, we watch in awe. "How do they do that?" is the most common response. The second most common is "I could never do that in a million years."

How *Do* They Do That?

Practice and more practice. Playfulness. Humor. Living "in the moment," plus focus and commitment to the scene and their fellow players. Their motivation? A big fat paycheck and the adoration of millions. In this book, we'll show you how you can translate those ideals to your life and work. No, we do not ask you to become an improvisational actor or a comedian on stage. (Believe us, there are too many of them out there—they don't need any more competition.) What we do ask you to believe, however, is that you are a performer on stage in life—at home, at work, and at play, all the time. And embracing the ideals and using the tools of improvisation in your life and career will help you not to become the next Drew Carey, Mike Myers, or Rosie O'Donnell, but to become simply more of you. Much more. And your motivation? The adoration of your coworkers and cohabitants, a more spontaneous, creative, in-the-moment life, and oh yeah, a bigger fatter paycheck.

I Could Never Do That in a Million Years!

Improvise scenes on television in front of live studio audience? Maybe not. Joyously improvise the scenes of your life in front of the next staff meeting, client, sales prospect, husband, wife, significant or insignificant other? Absolutely! If you're willing to practice a little, have fun, and take some deliciously uncalculated risks.

So Okay, What Is Improvisation?

You would have to ask that, wouldn't you? Well, here goes. Improvisation is a process—*the process in which something new and exciting is created in a moment of spontaneity—a flash of discovery ignited by a spark of inspiration.* Now we hear you saying to yourself, "Whoa. That sounds a little too artsy for me." After all, "I'm the senior vice president of Internet Technology for a multinational software company. Planning and strategy is critical. Improvising is not." Or "I manage a sports and health center. I can't be spontaneous when I'm selling a prospective member on the benefits of the 'Gold' versus the 'Platinum' personal fitness plan." Or "I'm a cruise director. I've got no time for that spontaneity and creativity. I've got to plan a luau on deck for nine hundred insurance agents, and we're in the middle of Hurricane Britney!" Or "I'm a woman with a career and a mother of three. I do improvise—I make three school lunches out of two crusts of bread and a slice of old baloney from an empty refrigerator. I'm an hour late for work and I think up a variation on the 'cat vomited on my laptop' excuse for my missing marketing report as I put on my mascara at 45 miles per hour."

Well, we are here to impress upon you that not only are the above life moments exactly the time to embrace the spirit of improvisation, but that spontaneity and creativity should be a way-of-life goal for each of us every day. "Too artsy?" Think of your life as a work of art in progress! It is, isn't it? And, have you ever improvised? Of course you have. Think back on all those times in your life when you experienced that personal spark of inspiration—whether in a crisis or in a contented mo-ment—that led you into the uncharted waters of discovery. The discovery of a solution to a problem, large or small. That flash of discovery of something new about yourself, or about another person, or about the world, when you were really "in the zone," or as we say—"in the moment"!

What Improvisation Is Not

As we explore how you can become more spontaneous and creative in your career and life through the ideals of improv, here's a caution on what improvisation is *not*. Improvising, as we see it, is not about being funny, being clever, or cracking jokes. In fact, in the theatrical improvisation in which we have many years of experience, we stress to actors that humor should only be the byproduct of an improvised scene. It is certainly not the goal. So, we say to you, the fun is in connecting with your spontaneous spirit—the pressure's off to be funny.

Also, to be a great improviser is not to be a fake improviser. True improvisation is in no way, shape, or form planned. It is by nature spontaneous and unrehearsed. The difference is easily recognized. For example, chatty local news anchors are notorious for "off-the-cuff" banter that is read directly off the TelePrompTer. What you are seeing is not bad improvisation. It's bad writing. Al Gore's heavy sighs, and his "spontaneous" walk up to invade G. W. Bush's personal space during the presidential debates were planned strategies debated for hours behind closed doors.

On the other hand, some may remember this wonderful true improvised moment in the vice-presidential campaign debate of 1988: When then Sen. Dan Quayle made the colossal mistake of comparing himself to John F. Kennedy, Sen. Lloyd Bentsen reacted with the now classic improvised comeback, "Senator, I served with Jack Kennedy, I knew Jack Kennedy, Jack Kennedy was a friend of mine. Senator, you are no Jack Kennedy." (Shouts and applause.) Point, set, match—improvised.

Now, how did he do it? How will you do it? Excellent questions. We invite you to take a deep breath and read on. It's time to introduce you to the ideals and tools you'll need as an improviser.

THE IDEALS OF IMPROVISATION

To become an effective improviser day in and day out—trusting your instincts and improvising boldly in life—means that you're ready and willing to commit to become very good at the following. Drum roll, please:

Take your job seriously and yourself lightly

Play

Say "Yes . . . And!"
(in a "No!" world)

Trust your gut

Live in the moment

You're onstage improvising every day of your life—
Commit to every scene

Trust yourself and those with whom you work and live

Have fun all the time

Take Your Job Seriously and Yourself Lightly

There is a lot to be serious about in this world: birth, disease, death, religion, your 401(k), and picking just the right tune for your cell phone to play when it rings. And, when it comes to your job, stakes are high, deadlines are inhumanly short, and you're on call and online nights, weekends, and any other available waking moment.

Of course you need to take what you do seriously, whether you're an ER physician or a window and door salesperson. But taking yourself lightly is about personal attitude. We're asking you to unclench your teeth and smile—to look at how you respond to your world and your work through "improv-colored glasses" and to see the humor. (Humor equals perspective!) Look into your own private personality mirror and see a grin instead of a grimace. And mean it. Every day. When you do, congratulations. You're now in the right frame of mind to—

Play!

All the theory and practice of improvising is based on a simple idea and the opposite of "work." Play. Yes, Play. Like a kid. Unstructured play is the ultimate spontaneous, creative atmosphere. The spirit of childlike play is at the root of being able to improvise. Build sandcastles on the beach, not the next great marketing paradigm. (In fact, building a sandcastle on the beach may lead you to the next great marketing paradigm.) Have you ever heard the expression "work to win"? Of course not. It's "play to win!"

Obvious an idea as it may seem, engaging in play may be an endangered practice, for adults, as well as children. In a *Time* magazine article,★ "What Ever Happened to Play?" it's noted that play is "joyful, and emotionally nourishing." Stuart Brown, a retired psychiatrist and founder of the Institute of Play in Carmel Valley, California, believes that too little play may have a dark side. What Brown calls "play deprivation" can lead, he says, to "depression, hostility and the loss of 'the things that make us human beings.' "

We agree. And so, the improvisation training sessions we lead around the country for businesses and individuals are play-based, in-the-moment interaction. They're not referred to as "workshops." We've renamed them "playshops," because to become a great improviser, there's no work allowed.

Say "Yes . . . And!" (in a "No!" World)

This idea is so shockingly important to us that we've devoted an entire chapter to it in the book. Here's a taste. Simply put,

---

★Kirnwith, Walter, and Wendy Cole. "What Ever Happened to Play?" *Time* (April 30, 2001): 56, 57, 58.

the concept of "Yes . . . And!" means this: Say "Yes" to your own idea or someone else's idea, and accept it no matter how "out there" or "been-there-done-that" it seems. Embrace another's idea as the best thought you've ever heard expressed in the history of humankind.

Then, add the all-important "And!"—add to their idea by supporting it and then add your own creative thoughts. Agree, and then together build on it. To say "Yes" means you are willing to suspend your judgment and discover something new—just to see where it might take you, to explore the unknown. To say "No" brings any moment to a screeching halt. Be honest with yourself. Are you usually a "Yes . . . And!" person or a "No!" person?

Go with Your Gut

How many times has a great (or small) spontaneous idea welled up in your throat ready to burst forth in all its glory, only to be swallowed and the moment allowed to pass into oblivion, because you either prejudged your idea's effect on the boss, or you just knew you'd either be greeted with gales of laughter or stunned and confused silence by your spouse? Sound familiar? *Webster's* defines "gut" as, among other things, "daring, courage, perseverance, vigor . . . power, or force." In improvising, we define "trust your gut" as the courage to go with your first impulse and damn the consequences—to have the presence of mind to shoot from the hip, when deep inside you know it's right. Dare to take a leap of faith with your idea, your thought, and your moment.

Okay, going with your gut doesn't always mean you've made the right choice. And there are consequences to every action.

(See previous *Titanic* analogy.) But chances are you're not piloting an oceanliner in iceberg-infested waters or performing laser eye surgery on the pope. That's not to belittle real-life consequences of going with your gut and blurting out "Susan, I realize you're my boss and this is a staff meeting, but I just have to say that you look like a zeppelin in that dress." Appropriateness in any given situation is always a factor. Indeed, a critical part of a from-the-gut improvised response involves paying attention to your own appropriateness radar. However, many of us tend to confuse this issue with fear. Our internal editor says, "I know what I'd like to say, but it's not appropriate because Susan already feels that her idea is the best idea. I'll be shot down if I speak up with my opinion." Remember, there are also consequences of inaction. And 90 percent of those awful things you think will happen just never do. Trusting your gut and acting on what it tells you leads you to more freedom, more discoveries, more fun, and more improvisation.

Live "In the Moment"

"Being there." "In the now." "In the zone." When the future Hall of Fame NFL receiver Chris Carter of the Minnesota Vikings caught his record-breaking one-thousandth pass, he described the experience as being able to actually "see the revolutions of the ball turning" while the football was in the air. Pro golfers explain that on those special days when they are "in the zone," their tiny golf ball appears to be the size of a basketball, and the hole on the green, the size of a garbage pail. Living "in the moment" creates a laser beam focus on the task or situation at hand in a world full of distractions, no matter what your profession.

Let's take a less highly paid, high-profile moment: You're a customer service manager in the middle of a client recovery crisis. In chapter 4, we'll dive along with you into methods to hone this same ability to relax, focus your mind and body to live exclusively in the moment. Your enhanced ability to be present, to actively listen to your agitated client and really understand his or her stated (and often unstated) concerns will lead more often than not to a highly effective response or a truly creative solution from you.

You're Onstage Improvising Every Day of Your Life— Commit Yourself to Every Scene

Throughout this book we ask you to accept the notion that you are indeed performing and improvising on the stage of life each day. It's an effective analogy for us to use and for you to envision when we discuss and analyze "life scenes" at the office or in a personal relationship. When the proverbial curtain goes up, the most dynamic and creative stage actors approach each performance as unique. They are in the moment, believing that they are saying their lines for the very first time. (Yes. Even if they're in the middle of their 1,557th night of *Cats*.) The result is that each performance they give on any given night has new qualities—it's fresh and alive.

In the very same sense, when using the skills of an improviser you have the opportunity to approach each new scene of your life (yes, even though it's the 1,557th night of your marriage), living in the moment, saying "Yes . . . And!" and working together to create something new and exciting. Improvising.

Trust Yourself and Those with Whom You Work and Live

Many times improvising in life is a group effort—a collaborative process. As improvisers on stage must trust their fellow actors to support them and their ideas, say "Yes . . . And!" and advance the scene, you must also suspend judgment and preconceived notions of those with whom you work and live in order to build an environment of trust in which spontaneity and creativity can flourish. For instance, as your colleague Bill drones on and on during the budget meeting, your thought process may be locked into a preconceived idea of who Bill is and what he's doing—for the twentieth time: "Here he goes again. Bill's just doing his usual smoke and mirrors act with his department's budget numbers . . . kissing butt, and making himself look good."

Well, it very well may be true. And maybe you can't stand Bill! However, if you can learn to take the leap and try to see Bill (the jerk) in a new and positive light each and every meeting, to trust him as a valuable part of this meeting "scene," spontaneity and creativity can occur. After all, you're in this scene together. And you have the power to turn this exercise in idiocy into a brand new scene. Listen.

React to Bill as if it's the first time you've ever met. Trust that he is the greatest scene/meeting partner you've ever had—and allow the possibility that creative sparks may fly from there. Trust us. It works.

Have Fun All the Time

Why not? What choice is there? Playfulness and a light spirit keep you young, healthy, creative, and in touch with the best in people and the world. Yes, you can have fun at work and still take the work seriously. Yes, you can build an environment of fun and play at home and in your personal life and still go to church and pay the bills. Make a personal commitment to have fun all the time.

And if you get in trouble, tell them we made you do it.

Those are the ideals. Here are the tools . . . Well, you're saying, "It's all fine and good to know the ideals—the goals. But how am I going to get there?" A fair question. However, one of the tools that we use to become a proficient theatrical improviser is applicable here: "Avoid questions. Make declarations." Questions tend to throw the responsibility for creativity on another's shoulders. To make a "declaration" is to make a bold statement. But, you didn't know that. So, in the spirit of "Yes . . . And!" let's begin again. "Yes," those are the ideals, "And!" here is a brief overview of the tools and skills you will soon use to audaciously improvise the scenes of your life:

Make Declarations: Make courageous personal statements of intent in your relationships and daily interactions— and then act upon them.

Explore and Heighten: Explore all possibilities in your personal moments, make daring discoveries, and take them farther than you ever thought possible.

Give and Take: Master the flowing process of "giving focus" and "taking focus" in the scenes of your life—in a relationship, in your family, with a client or business partner.

Actively Listen: Blank out outside stimuli, including your own negative thoughts and judgment, and listen with your entire body.

Be More of That—Be More of You: Find what is intuitively important to you or in what you excel—and make a strong commitment to "do more of that" or "become more of that."

So that's what improvisation is. Got it? Great. Let's do it.

IMPROVISATION EXERCISES: IF EVERYONE DOES IT, NO ONE LOOKS LIKE AN IDIOT!

The Experience

All right, "Why do these exercises at all?" you ask. Here's why—their strength lies in your mind and body working together. You need to *experience* what it feels like to improvise. It is not enough to just get the concept intellectually.

Would you rehearse a speech without saying your incredibly well-written words aloud? Learn a foreign language without moving your lips? Learn how to mambo without moving your hips? Of course not! Many of these simple improvisation exercises have a physical element incorporated in them. Get up. Move around. Jump around. Laugh. Cry. Scream! Remember, the body tends to remember what the mind forgets.

The Atmosphere

It's one of "play." (There's that word again.) We'll also refer to these exercises as "games." View them as a process, a learning experience—freeflowing and free of judgment (there's no "right" or "wrong"). For many of the individual improvisation exercises throughout the book it's important to find your own quiet, comfortable play space. Pick a time when you're not rushed so you can pay full attention to the game at hand and enjoy the ride. Finally, consider a playing partner. A close friend is fine. A child is even better. If you don't have one, borrow one. Children have not yet lost the knack for leaping into an entertaining game at the drop of a hat. They're for the most part supportive and are young masters at the art of saying "Yes . . . And!"

The primary goal is unadulterated fun, which we believe is the ultimate learning atmosphere. If it's not fun, it's work. (Remember—no work allowed.) If these games become work, you might as well be back in the cubicle with a spreadsheet, a copy of *Windows for Dummies,* and a Little Debbie's Snack Cake.

Lather. Rinse. Repeat.

The first time out with any of these games may be frustrating. Even more frustrating if you think in terms of immediate results. Play the game. Work yourself into a lather. (Commit to it.) Rinse your mind and body. (Shake it off after each attempt.) And Repeat. (Do it again and again!) Unlike the Richard Simmons "Sweating to the Oldies" workout tape that's gathering dust on your shelf, perform these exercises as often as you can. Remember, if you were trying to do the splits for the first time in your life, you wouldn't attempt it the first day, would you? Your body might need days or weeks of stretching. (Personally, we would need years, and a good surgeon.) If you did try to do the splits on the first day, you'd probably pull a muscle.

If you are trying to change your life through improvisation, your mind needs to be stretched slowly with these exercises. Don't pull a mental muscle on the first day! Build on your experience by repetition. Progress, understanding, and change are in the doing.

Journal It!

A key to cement the improvisation exercises and drills into your psyche is to reflect on them in writing after the fact. Keep an official *Improvise This!* journal. You'll find that many of your most useful statements can begin with the phrases "I observed that . . ." and "I felt that . . ." Refer back to it often as you chart your path and your progress.

Finally, as you begin to tone your creative mental physique, you'll gain the confidence to improvise more and more. And you will begin to apply these techniques to your day-to-day life without even knowing it.

The Result?

For example, you may find yourself:

- Taking more (calculated) risks in expressing your ideas during a meeting.
- Feeling more comfortable when speaking to a group of peers, whether at church, at the city council meeting, or at your inauguration.
- Replacing fear with a new sense of confidence in your ability to challenge and change old patterns of behavior and thought.
- Explaining to your spouse over the sky phone on the Concorde en route to Paris that you just had to "go with your gut" and take a master class from Marcel Marceau in "Miming for Managers."
- Performing the scenes of your life with energy and a stronger point of view.
- Saying "Yes" to the playful, childlike, spontaneous part of you that's tucked away behind the "I shoulds" and "I have to follow the script."

IMPROVISE THIS!

PERSONAL EXERCISE 1
A Week's Worth of Play

The Players: You and your imagination.

The Object: Begin your week by setting the goal of *trying seven new things*. Think of it as taking the risk to finally try that radically new hairstyle you've secretly been thinking about. "Try on" new actions, new behaviors, new mannerisms, and new ways of saying things to see how they "fit."

How To:
1. Sing in the shower. First, a favorite song. Now make up a song. Rhyme it.

2. Eat a completely different lunch at a brand-new restaurant. Just because.

3. Get dressed as though you've just won the lottery, and you're on your way to pick up the check.

4. Recite a poem to your family at the dinner table. (Hell, they already think you're weird for making up songs in the shower . . .)

5. Say the ABCs out loud in the car on the way home from work. In slow motion. Savor every letter, as if it were Shakespeare.

6. Spend a day of the weekend noticing *EVERYTHING*, as if you'd just popped out of the womb

and were seeing the world for the very first time. Take extra time to notice the specific taste and smell of food. Can you list each ingredient by the flavor? What does the smell of that chicken soup remind you of? Observe your children's features in detail, as a portrait artist would—the tones in their skin and the shapes of their necks. Pay attention to exactly where the newspaper is tossed in the morning, the way a squirrel in the yard leaps, and the color of your spouse's socks—take time to notice *EVERYTHING*.

7. Pantomime.

Option One (Simple): Take an imaginary drink of water. First, envision your own kitchen. Really see it in your mind's eye. In detail. Now, walk up to the imaginary cupboard, open it, and take out a glass. Feel its color, size, and weight. Now move to the imaginary sink, turn the faucet, and fill the glass. Take a drink. How does it taste? Is the water cold? Lukewarm? Salty? Finally, go to your actual kitchen and repeat the same pattern. How did it differ from your imaginary glass of water? Feeling ridiculous? Good. Time to feel even more ridiculous! Repeat the exercise in slow motion, and try to create twice the detail.

Option Two (More Challenging): Open an imaginary Christmas present. Don't preplan what is in the box. Take your time with the ribbons and wrapping. Now open and look in. Visualize the gift exactly. Now pick it up. Notice the weight, texture, and color. Now use the gift. If it's a sweater, put it on. If it's a CD, put it in the imaginary CD player and start dancing to the music. Take your time. Really. We're not kidding.

Finally, each day in your journal, record the action you took, and how it made you feel. Did you enjoy it? Did it make you feel silly? Why? What did you learn from this week? How can it help you become more of who you are?

The Result: The best actors, the best improvisers are keen observers of the nuances of the life around them. As you complete these exercises, you will feel an increased sensitivity to how you act, how you imagine, and the specific colors, textures, and tones of the world around you. When you begin to observe ordinary occurrences through a sharper lens, you are on your way to using the same powers of observation to truly see and use the details of your life in a new way.

BREAKING BARRIERS

Take a Flying Leap Over the Wall of Fear

Twelve magicians and two carnies have been shot dead doing
the bullet catch. That's cool enough, but every night when we
close our show with that trick and the loaded gun gets pointed
in my face, it goes so far beyond cool. All I can think is, twelve
magicians, two carnies.

—Penn Jillette, of Penn & Teller

So. How did you feel when you did those exercises? Silly?
Good. Energized? Even better. Are you ready to jump on the
stage of your life and take a risk, say, "Yes!" and "catch a bullet"
at your morning staff meeting? If so, you're on your way . . . But
wait a minute. Be honest. Did you actually do the exercises? Or,
have you decided to put them off for a few chapters and maybe

someday stick a tentative toe in the water when you have the time? Well, it's perfectly fine to be feeling hesitant right now. Understandable. After all, change is hard. However, the time is now to screw up your courage and jump in the icy waters of improvisation. It's a cold shock at first, but before you know it, you'll be swimming like a fish. (Shark? Bass? Walleyed pike? We'll leave that up to you.)

In **Breaking Barriers** we're about to take a gander at the most common obstacles we place in our own paths that stop us from having the confidence to embrace, practice, and enjoy the life-stretching experience of improvising. Here they are: first, there's fear. And then there's . . . fear. And oh yeah, there's fear. Consider this:

THE TELEVISION DRAMA OF YOUR LIFE

Fade-in after commercial.

Location: Your Life.

You are revealed pacing the floor of your home, apartment, or office.

The HOST of the TV drama of your life—a man who looks suspiciously like Rod Serling—walks slowly into frame and looks into the camera. He speaks:

HOST: Hello. Today is a day like any other day . . . Well, except like yesterday, which was nuts . . . It's a typical day in the life of [insert your name here]. [Your name] is happy. Life is sweet. Because life is—predictable. Or is it? [Your name] is about to make the decision of his/her life. To take a risk. [Your name] doesn't know it, but he/she's about to leave . . . "The Comfort Zone!"

Strange music suspiciously like the theme from *The Twilight Zone* swells to a crescendo.

Have you seen that episode? Chances are it's already playing in the reruns of your psyche. Fear, of course, is at the root of moving beyond what we know (our comfort zone) into the unknown.

The best improvisers—like the best technicians, auto mechanics, schoolteachers, billionaire/bankrupt Internet start-up company twenty-eight year olds, and the best companies—have one thing in common: the confidence to take the personal or business risks that allow them the opportunity to succeed. They are the chance takers, the go-for-brokers, and the "I'd rather apologize for what I did, than what I didn't do" improvisers. We're drawn to them. We wonder at their guts and their seeming lack of concern for consequences. They seem to travel on a different path from the straight-and-narrow types—they're whooping it up on life's roller-coaster ride to the unknown, instead of safely heading down the old straight-and-narrow for another afternoon at the strip mall. They are in many important ways, fearless.

TAKE A FLYING LEAP OVER THE WALL OF FEAR

I am the lizard king. I can do anything.

—Jim Morrison, the Doors

Jim Morrison of the Doors was fearless. And a genius. He was also seriously chemically challenged. Now, we're not asking you to bare your soul and your posterior in front of an audience and get arrested, as did Jim. But he exhibited (among other things) utter confidence in that act, because he knew he was good. He was an amazing singer and songwriter. Jim Morrison took many small steps along his path to become the best he could possibly be. He became "more of himself."

Of course, then he crashed and burned. But you get the point.

Small steps lead to great leaps. It's time to take a jump down from the rock-god pedestal onto the stage of your life, and talk about five small concrete steps you can take on your journey to become a risk-taker and a fearless improviser. It all begins when you make the choice to change. Then, add a little self-examination, playfulness, and commitment to try—which will lead you to a healthy measure of self-confidence and growth. We promise. Improvise this if you will:

FIVE SMALL STEPS

1. Discover one thing in your life you are good at—"Yes" yourself.
2. Declare your intention and passion to be the best at it—Make a declaration.
3. Take a risk and a next step—"Yes . . . And!" yourself.
4. Heighten your actions—Just be more of you.
5. Take your actions farther than you believed possible—Be even more of you.

Small Step 1—"Yes" Yourself

To begin, ask yourself this question: "What is one positive thing I'm really good at in my life?" If your answer is a resounding "Nothing," seek therapy and possibly medication. Short of that, take a few moments then to listen carefully to those in your life whose opinions you trust—your life-scene partners. Ask the above question to your best friend, a family member, or a colleague with whom you've worked closely for eight years at the office. Really listen to what they say you're good at. Chances are they're right on the money. Make sense? Good. Or, if your confident answer is "Yes, I'm not only good but great at so many things—it's hard to choose," it's time to make a list. It might look something like this:

My Yes List

- Yes, I am a good father.
- Yes, I am a dynamite accountant.
- Yes, I play a mean game of racquetball.
- Yes, I am a thoughtful neighbor.
- Yes, I'm incredible at procrastinating. I haven't cleaned the inside of the refrigerator since the collapse of the Soviet Union . . . (Scratch that one—remember "positive.")
- Yes, my barbeques are a family legend.

All right, a fine list. Now, since "Yes, my barbeques are a family legend" is simple yet there's a lot of meat to it, let's work with your summer outdoor cooking prowess as the prime example.

Small Step 2—Make a Declaration

In a booming voice, declare to yourself "I am the barbeque king!" Say it again. And again. Believe it. Yes, positive reinforcement works. Remember, we define the improvisation tool of making declarations as the art and practice of making courageous personal statements of intent, and acting upon them. The natural tendency is to be tentative. Have courage. Commit to it. "I am the barbeque king!" Following this internal dialogue, it's time to make the declaration public with the same sense of assurance to your family and friends. There's nothing wrong and everything right with being proud of your expertise and announcing it firmly to the world around you.

When you've accomplished this, congratulations. You've now declared to yourself and to the world your unparalleled excellence in the art and practice of a great American institution—barbeque.

Small Step 3—"Yes . . . And!" Yourself

And . . . ? Now, here comes an important personal leap of faith: "Yes, I am the barbeque king, and I am going to develop my talent further by finally taking that gourmet cooking class, Grilling Your Way to Gastronomic Greatness." You sign up. You get even better. Swordfish, shrimp, and salmon are now menu items added to your incredible burgers, dogs, and brats. You invite the Johnsons from the apartment across the street, and the Catholic couple and their seven children from next door. All are impressed—and full. The result? The barbeques are now a neighborhood legend. By embracing ". . . And!" you've moved from "good" to "very good."

Small Step 4—Just Be More of You

In theatrical improvisation it's critical to take the discoveries you have made about your character, the scene, and your relationship with the other players to the limit and beyond, if only to find out where they will lead. We call this technique "Just be more of that—just be more of you." Why not with your skills as a barbequer? (Or anything else you've chosen from the list of positive things at which you are good?) You've taken three small steps. It's time to take a couple more to make discoveries about your personal limitations and make the attempt to move beyond them, to sense and then to realize your possibilities. Here's how:

* You decide to treat your entire church group to one of your barbeques.
* Al, the baritone from the choir, loves your basted chicken so much he eats thirty-one pieces and leaves bloated, in an ambulance. You're shaken.
* After his stomach is pumped, however, Al calls you at your office the next morning. He's ecstatic about your food. Al gives you the name of a venture capitalist he knows in New York (Ms. Kim), who specializes in developing new restaurant chains throughout the Pacific Rim.
* Spending a sleepless night, repeating over and over to yourself, "Yes . . . And . . . Yes, I'm the barbeque king, a family and neighborhood legend, and I'd like to be swimming in money like my ribs are in sauce!" You place the call to Ms. Kim the next morning, and . . .

And several things may happen. You never get past her secretary. Or, Ms. Kim herself demurs and says, "Thanks, but no thanks." Or, she tells you that she's aching to put together a mammoth start-up deal for you; you catch the next flight to La Guardia and become a millionaire restaurateur overnight. Or, after considering all the options, you realize you've taken your skill and talent in cooking about as far as you want to go. Or, or, or . . . The possibilities are endless. The single reality is, however, no matter what the end result you have not failed—in any sense of the word. In fact, you have grown. (Look where you were in step 1!) The only failure is in not making the attempt, in saying "No" when your gut tells you to say "Yes!" You've become "more of you."

Small Step 5—Be Even More of You

Ask yourself this question: "How far do I want to take it?" In reality, your wonders-with-the-Weber may simply lead you to a very happy family at dinnertime—and that's fine, provided that is the level at which you decide your cooking creativity and talent will reside. Why is this journey important? Simply because the wonderfully positive improviser in you has decided to take the risk. You explored your talent, and heightened it—and now you can choose to heighten it yet again and become even more of you, which will create new possibilities, new realities and opportunities in your life. It's your decision.

The Great Leap

Of course you could have stopped at any step along the way and chalked it up to fear. Fear of rejection, of appearing foolish, of financial risk—fear of making (heaven forbid) a mistake! Now, these are very real fears we all face along the life-improviser's path. However, it's important to consider this: We *all* have these anxieties! And, we all must make the affirming choice to live with, manage, and overcome our fears, large and small in all areas of our life. In *Feel the Fear and Do It Anyway,* author Susan Jeffers passes along these truths: "The only way to get rid of the fear of doing something is to go out . . . and do it." And, "Not only am I going to experience fear whenever I'm on unfamiliar territory, but so is everyone else." Finally, "Pushing through fear is less frightening than living with the underlying fear that comes from a feeling of helplessness."

As a new improviser, each time you embrace and push through the next small risk and then the next, and the next, you become more confident in playing the improvised scenes of your life to the hilt. You've become the "barbeque king of the world" (or of the square city block of your neighborhood). It might have been "accountant of the century" or "father of the universe." The important point is that before you know it, you will have jumped in the water, improvised these five small steps, and taken a great leap—from declaring yourself good at one particular part of your life, to realizing your potential to become amazing at it.

THE IMPROVISER'S NIGHTMARE

> You lose the need to judge yourself . . . The lesson is: Don't be afraid to go out and risk it. The tragedy is to play it safe.
> —"Number of Corporate Drones Sent Off to Improv Class," *The Wall Street Journal,* June 15, 1999

Recently the head of corporate training for a large health-care company in California said this as she spoke to us just a few days before our full day workshop with hundreds of top executives, "Oh, by the way, I purposely left out any mention in our conference agenda that your seminar is on improvisation." When we asked the somewhat stunned, and inevitable, "Why?" she replied, "It would make them much too nervous."

Doctors, nurses, and hospital administrators who face disease and death (the ultimate in customer care) and meet yawning black chasms of budget bottom lines with ease are "too nervous" to learn how to improvise?

Well, of course they are nervous. Many executives (like many of us) who get a whiff of the notion that "improv" is about to occur in a business workshop setting too often have this frightening image flashing in his or her head: "I will be standing on stage in front of my peers, about to perform like a dancing bear—without a script, TelePrompTer, or agenda, stripped of my job title suit of armor and outfitted only with my own personality and wit. I will be commanded to be funny. I will freeze. I will fail. I will be judged and condemned."

This premonition of personal meltdown has been known for years in the performing business as "the actor's nightmare." In this case it's been transformed into "the executive's onstage-improv-seminar nightmare."

Well (affecting our best, soothing therapist's voice), it's okay to have a little anxiety mixed in with a healthy dose of stage fright right now. Especially as you begin to use improv in your career and with others whom you've cultivated a certain professional image. Take all the time you need for the ideals of improvisation to sink in and to feel comfortable enough to begin to practice what we preach.

All right, time's up.

Cut to: The same California health-care seminar, following the big breakfast buffet. Six corporate leaders, including the president, are coaxed from their seats, and find themselves onstage with tight smiles on their faces, staring into the lights and into the black hole of the first improvisation exercise of the day, "Everybody Go!" (See Group Exercise 2 in the Epilogue.)

After we coach them on how the exercise should flow, a senior vice president, let's call her Susan, steps to the front of the stage. The entire audience, instructed to do so, is on its feet expectantly watching only her. Time stands still.

It's the moment of truth, and the possible onset of the "executive's nightmare" for Susan. Now Susan has three choices:

She can say, "I can't do this," and politely move back in line. Or, she can take a little stab at it, make a safe, sound, and small physical motion and fulfill the letter of the exercise. Or she can . . . Here's what really happened: A crazy yowl bursts out of her mouth, as she simultaneously dances in a circle with her arms waving above her head. The entire audience of her peers shouts *"Yes!"* and three hundred voices immediately yowl back at her, bodies dancing in a circle en masse like a seriously warped preschool game of Simon Says.

Gales of laughter. Hundreds of tight smiles turn into grins. The next executive steps up to the front of the stage, ready to go. The first barrier was broken. Susan took a small step and embraced a personal moment of spontaneous combustion, which had a ripple effect throughout the entire audience. Her moment was a beginning—a small personal discovery.

The audience supported her (said "Yes!") and confidence to improvise grew in each succeeding person on stage. (Small steps lead to great leaps.) And guess what? The rest of the day pretty much took care of itself.

The point of the above truth-is-funnier-than-fiction seminar story is this: The California health-care company needed to explore a fresh approach to the personal well-being of their leaders. Facing job stress and the responsibility of a very serious corporate mission, the company felt the need to take some time to reignite the spirit of their leaders. We were there to motivate pharmacists, doctors, nurse administrators, and hospital heads to have fun and to help guide each individual to explore something brand new, using the ideals and practice of improvisation.

Together they bolted over a collective corporate wall of fear. First, they took the chance to introduce improvisation into their serious world. Second, with our help, the company created an atmosphere where play and spontaneity and having a good time was not only allowed, but also encouraged. This atmosphere is a key. Knowing that the attendees were coming in blind to the fact that they were about to be introduced to improvisation, we made a point to create a group feeling of play by performing a satirical sketch about their company, and performing improvised scenes ourselves and with their participation. Once the group felt like they then had the permission to play and were not being judged, almost every individual gave the experience his or her best shot.

And what was their risk? Looking stupid? Declining profits? Loopy neurosurgeons exclaiming "Hey, I feel like improvising today—let's have a little fun during this procedure while I'm taking the pressure off this guy's cerebellum!" No. The only risk was that they might have a great time that day, learn a lot about themselves, and bring that positive feeling back to work.

You can bring that positive feeling into your personal world. What's your risk? Rejection? Ridicule? Failure? No. We contend that the only risk is that you might love what it really feels like to be a life-improviser so much that you sell the furniture and the SUV, start an improv troupe, and start performing marathon midnight shows in Central Park.

TIPS ON THE TOPIC

It Feels Good. So do it. We'll say it again—improvising is all in the doing. To help you recognize that old improv feeling when you've stopped beating your head against that wall of fear and push through, allowing the wall to just disappear, here are some typical comments from theatrical improvisers of all types and stripes as they've broken through their own personal barriers. (Referring to these as you play through the improvisation exercises is especially helpful.)

"I was so frustrated. I swore to myself that I would work and work until I 'got it.' Turns out, I didn't get it. I was in my head for a long time trying to think improvisation to death. Then one afternoon in class, I kind of gave up, and just watched, listened, and played. It worked."

"Time seemed to slow down to a crawl when I was really there—in the moment!"

"After the workshop I noticed that my whole body had become incredibly relaxed and quiet."

"I felt like I had become one big antenna, tuned in to absolutely everything around me."

"When I finally got it through my thick head that nothing I did in the exercises was wrong, I really started to have fun."

"I forgot about myself and focused completely on the other person—just listened and reacted. Improvising seemed easy."

Now, Get on with It

Now that you know how to break a few barriers and use our five small steps to "just be more of you," have at it. Never fear. Or, never let fear get the best of you. To take the risk to say, "Yes!" to yourself and to those around you is to laugh at the unknown and to embrace it for what it is—an opportunity to shine, to discover a new way to approach your business or

personal relationships, to make it up as you go along. Hey—
to improvise!

> The first step toward playing is feeling personal freedom.
>
> —Viola Spolin, *Improvisation for the Theater*

PERSONAL EXERCISE 2
Walk in Space

Players: You guessed it. Just you.

The Object: To bust out of your physical boundaries and "I-have-to-act-this-way-because-I'm-an-adult" patterns.

How To: Find a relatively large open room where you can move freely and make strange noises. A recreation room or a basement will do (or a bus station, where no one will notice your strange behavior, anyway). Suit yourself.
Note: Start slowly. If you find some of the steps below are too difficult at first, begin with step 1 through step 4, and repeat. When you've mastered this pattern, play with the entire sequence!

1. First, walk around the room casually. Head up. Eyes front. As if you are walking into a cocktail party.

2. Begin walking faster. You're late for work.

3. Now in slow motion. Visualize that you're wading through a vat of thick pudding.

4. Break into skipping.

5. As you skip, make a loud repetitive sound with each step.

6. Now switch to ballroom dancing with an imaginary partner. Hum as loud as you can as you swirl. (You think this is absolutely ridiculous, don't you? That's the point!)

7. Stop—look at the wall and talk as fast as you can about what you see in the room.

8. Hunch over and become as small as you can. Begin to hop around as this new "tiny you."

9. Repeat in a random pattern.

10. Make up your own crazy patterns.

11. Stop and check the door again to make sure it's locked.

The Result: An absolute necessity in improvisation is to lose your physical inhibitions, which improves your ability to listen to and use your body. "Walk in Space" will help you get in tune with this, creating a more free and supple mind and body.

AN INSIDE TIP FROM OUTSIDE THE BOX

This is the first in a series of inspirational interviews that will take you deep into the (sometimes seriously warped) minds of experienced improvisers from diverse backgrounds. Each shares his or her views on how improv has affected their work, their play, and their private relationships. With all, improvisation has become a large barrier-breaking part of their approach to life—as we hope it will be for you.

Dr. Jim Robinson

Jim Robinson has a Ph.D. in Psychology from the University of Southern California. He is currently a professor at the College of St. Catherine and St. Thomas in St. Paul, Minnesota, where he teaches general psychology, abnormal psychology, and counseling techniques, among other subjects. Dr. Robinson is also an experienced clinical therapist. (Not fun, but very important.) In addition, Jim has been a student, actor, and teacher of improvisation for the past nine years. (Fun and also important.)

Q: Jim, we have to ask. What made you take the leap from being in academia to trying an improvisation class?

A: *Well, I was about to turn thirty, and I was in graduate school for the second time. I looked in the newspaper and saw ads for improv classes in L.A. I've always been an introverted person and I thought, If I don't try this, I'll regret it. So, I thought I'd take one class and see what it was like.*

Q: So, what was it like?

A: *I got there an hour early. I was sick to my stomach. I was sweating. Terrified the whole time. It was eight weeks of absolute torture.*

Q: Ouch. If it was so painful, why did you stay with it?

A: *It did show me that I could do something utterly terrifying, and do it over and over and get better at it. It was a great class, despite the terror. The instructor, Cynthia Szigeti, was a huge influence on me.*

Q: So you continued taking improvisation classes?

A: *Yes. When I moved to Minneapolis, the next improv class I took wasn't focused on being funny, but being in the moment. I was on teams as a kid. Sports teams that I wasn't very good at. Here there was a team, an ensemble I could be in that I would actually enjoy.*

Q: What does improv have to do with a team? An ensemble?

A: *If it's pure improvisation, it's an ensemble activity. It's about making the scene look good and your fellow players look good. Saying "Yes" to whatever happens. When the fear of competition is removed, and the fear of judgment is removed, people go wild. When you get caught up in the moment and you're working together, you forget yourself.*

Q: And what did learning improvisation goals and tools do for you, outside "the team"?

A: *It changed my life. It really did. It gave me a point of view and a philosophy to follow that I didn't have before. Well, the one I had before was based on Christian day school and a lot of judgment.*

Q: Is there a key improvisation concept that you've taken to heart in your teaching career?

A: *The whole idea of a moment in improvisation is that it's the only moment you have. It's also the best moment you have. If you say "Yes" to what happens in that moment, then something incredible can happen that you certainly didn't plan. And, if you can ride with it, you're on to another moment, then another moment.*

    When I'm at my best, I'm not trying to control the moment; I'm just trying to respond. When I teach college psychology now, I do this all the time. Now [after improv training], I know if something goes wrong in class, if a student says something way off the mark, and if I work with that moment, it usually leads to something revealing, or deeper than what I was trying to get across.

Q: Wow. Really?

A: *Or it may be hogwash, but then we can laugh about it.*

Q: Many people, who would love to work or live a little more improvisationally or perhaps just want to be able to get up in front of an audience without a script, live in fear of "falling on their face." Thoughts?

A: *In [improv] class and onstage, there are moments when I am absolutely stuck, and the scene is dead. It happens all the time. But if you stay with it, something amazing happens. You get beyond all the "planning" and you get to the truth of the situation. Going through that wall of fear is the most satisfying feeling I can think of. And anybody can improvise. People who come at it from a non-acting background are even better, because they're not trying to act—they really are in the moment.*

Q: What about "Yes . . . And"?

A: *Some people have a very hard time saying, "Yes." They have to say "no" a thousand times before they say "yes." And when they say "yes" just once, that's all it takes.*

Q: Has it affected your personal life? If we may ask . . .

A: *I think of improv twenty hours a day it seems. It's the thing I love to do the most. Whenever I'm frustrated in a relationship, any moment is a possibility. If I say yes to certain things that I never said yes to before, things are better. And, my life-planning has changed some. I used to really force myself to plan things when I wasn't ready. I find now that I can tolerate "not knowing" and that ambiguity a lot more because of improv. Also, I needed to learn to have more fun. When I think about what I learned about improvising, I try to let go of my expectations and have a good time.*

Q: So, we gather it really has changed you. (For the better we hope.)

A: *The biggest change is that I ended up wanting to be an improvisation actor and a teacher and not a counselor. Eight years of graduate school down the drain. I've never looked back.*

Q: Where do you take improvisation from here?

A: *I'd like to keep performing, writing scripts, traveling. I'd love to keep both feet in improvising. I'd also like to have a solid relationship that would support me in every possible way.*

Q: Wouldn't we all. Last question, Jimmy. How about a final improvisation tip for our readers?

A: *Sure. I believe anyone can benefit, and anyone can do it.*

THREE

SPONTANEOUS COMBUSTION

Igniting Your Creative Spark

Some people have been known to spontaneously combust. Meaning they have literally burst into flames for no apparent reason. Personally, we believe it has something to do with Mexican food and corduroy slacks, but we can't prove it.

There is something else we cannot prove, but strongly believe. In improvisation there is a moment—an exact defining moment where all the proper conditions come together to ignite a spark of creativity. If this moment is recognized and seized, spontaneous combustion will occur and the momentum of that creative explosion will thrust the improvisation scene forward. If the moment is not recognized, the spark will go out, possibly taking the life of the scene with it.

Defining moments like these occur not only on the improvisation stage, they occur regularly on the stage of our personal and business lives. Unfortunately, we are often too busy to recognize them and let them work to our advantage. The spark goes out and we are left unfulfilled, scratching our heads wondering why we are stuck, wheels spinning, most of the time.

DID YOU SAY SPARK?

Thomas Alva Edison harnessed the power of electricity to create the electric lightbulb. Even more impressive was that Edison's imagination was sparked so often he holds more patents than any other single person in history— 1,093.

So, what is a creative spark? Think of a spark as an inspiration. An inspiration that causes you to take action, experience a heightened emotion, or expand your creative capacity. A spark can be as simple as:

- A beautiful sunset
- Two young girls playing jump rope
- An old leather bomber jacket
- A ladybug traversing a blade of grass

Now here's an example of what could happen when one of these sparks (the beautiful sunset) spontaneously combusts:

From the balcony outside her hotel room on the final day of the electronics trade show, Mary watches a magnificent and beautiful sunset. A tear of joy trickles down her cheek. Arriving home that next day she digs through the attic and pulls out the dust-ridden art supplies from her college days. She spends most of her free time the following week completing a painting inspired by that sunset. Mary then sends it to her old college roommate who is getting married the next month.

This little fable included each of the possible outcomes of an inspiration. The tear (heightened emotions), digging out the old painting supplies and using them (action), and using the painting as a unique and personal wedding gift (expanded creative capacity).

There is no set list of sparks, because different things inspire each of us. But always keep in mind: *A spark can never be manufactured; it can only be experienced.*

Now, before you run off and try to be inspired, why not just take a deep breath, clear your head and be very still. Good, now you're in the place where combustion can truly happen.

Finding the Quiet Place

In order to be in a position to combust, we must be very still and very quiet . . . in our minds. A quiet mind allows our focus to be laser sharp, to pick up on the slightest variance. If our focus is scattered, with energy going in many different directions, it becomes impossible to listen well or fully sense what is happening around us. And if we don't tap into our senses, we will miss many valuable opportunities to ignite a spark. And that one spark could open the door to valuable contributions and inspired solutions.

The ability to "get still" is not an innate one. We need to practice getting still and staying still. Try the following "Two Minute Improv Drill" and see just how sharp your focus can be

YOU KNOW THE IMPROV DRILL

Two-Minute Drill

Here's all you need: access to a radio and a set of headphones. Sit in a comfortable chair and tune in a radio station that you're not already familiar with. If you can find a radio talk show, that's even better. Now put on the headphones, close your eyes, listen—listen intently—and visualize what you're hearing. Imagine what the people look like; visualize the entire studio they are in, everything about it. After what seems like about two minutes unplug the headphones, open your eyes, and continue to listen for another two minutes. Continue to try to visualize as you did before. After two minutes return to the headphones, close your eyes, and once again, listen. Repeat this three times with the headphones on and three times without them.

when there are no outside influences and . . . when there are. After you've completed the drill spend some time digesting the experience. If you are like most people, you will see how much more difficult it is to focus, even for just two minutes, when there are potential distractions (headphones off). Note the rising level of frustration that accompanies being distracted. Also note how rich our imagination can be when we have fewer distractions and the sense of diminished frustration that comes with being able to focus.

Do you find your ability to focus compromised at work because of the numerous distractions you encounter? Do you think that these distractions, in turn, limit your ability to recognize those moments when a spark occurs? If so, here's what

you can do. Much like a quick mid-afternoon nap can revital-
ize your energy level, finding a couple of minutes where you
can be alone and "get still" can reinvigorate your focus mech-
anism, heighten your awareness, and help you get reconnected.
Try it . . . you'll like it.

Filling the Well

In addition to honing the ability to get still as part of your
combustion preparation, you also need to find means of con-
tinual nourishment . . . for the mind. It is very difficult to be
inspired by something of which you have little or no understanding or knowledge. That is not to say that new things
cannot inspire us, it only means we are not as likely to pick
up on the potential of something for which we have no point
of reference.

Simply put, the more information you have at your disposal,
the more likely you are to make connections with people and
therefore increase the possibility of creating a spark. Why do personal ads include information other than just, "Hey, I'm looking,
wanna get together?" Because the more we have in common, the
better chance there is for a spark. Yet in terms of spontaneous
combustion, it's more than just gathering endless information to
toss out in the hope that someone else knows about the dietary
habits of Romans in 454 B.C., therefore creating a spark.

It's actually about the comfort of familiarity. Take work, for
example. The more familiar you become with your work, the
more comfortable you are. The more comfortable you are, the
less you consternate about your ability to contribute, which in
turn, allows you to be more focused, more still, and ready to
combust. Our advice? Fill the "work well" too. Garner as much
knowledge as you can about where you work. It will give you

a richer perspective that will make you more productive and combustible in the long run.

- Who founded the company you work for and why?
- What are the products, services, and campaigns that never left the ground?
- Who are inspired employees and what have they accomplished over the years?

In order to learn about things outside of our normal stream of information, to better fill the "personal well," here are a few suggestions of what improvisers do, and you can too:

- When wandering through the bookstore at the airport, grab a magazine you would likely never purchase (men: *Tiger Beat*; women: *Soldier of Fortune*) and look through it for five minutes.
- When channel surfing some night stop on a channel that you always buzz right by and watch for a while. Foreign language stations are great.
- At the mall, stop in and browse through stores you don't normally shop. Pick up a few different items and feel them, smell them—be thorough.
- Take back roads instead of the usual route.

Not only will these information dumps increase your breadth of knowledge, which can be personally satisfying and make you a top-notch trivia buff, but at work you will be able to attack problems from more varied angles and see more possibilities for combustion in any situation. Who knows, taking that back road might be the spark that ends up as the backdrop for your ad agency's award-winning car commercial.

Just the Right Conditions

A flame cannot exist in a vacuum. Nor can creativity. As we speak of the elements necessary for spontaneous combustion to occur, we must examine our surroundings to see if they are conducive to spontaneous combustion. The following sets of goals and conditions are *not* supportive and therefore, incompatible:

- Starting a campfire with damp wood on damp ground.
- Delivering a PowerPoint presentation in an extremely bright room.
- Wearing a necktie while playing golf.

Whatever it is you are trying to accomplish, your setting must support your mission. To accomplish spontaneous combustion you must: 1) Find your internal quiet place; 2) fill your personal well; and 3) cultivate the perfect conditions.

I See It . . . I See It . . .

You've filled the well and your mind's as still as a statue when it finally happens. The spark. And you see it, as bright as a busfull of MENSA students. It's the mother of all inspirations. So, what do you do now? Good question. It depends on whether you've cultivated your "right conditions." These people have:

- The musical lyricist who has a ready supply of pen and paper on the bedside stands to capture thoughts before drifting off to sleep.
- The large corporation that replaced every fluorescent light with softer incandescent light to add warmth to their building.
- The jogger, who while training for the Boston Marathon, changed his daily route to include a pass by the park midway through his run. The reason? The park has four bright and shiny new portajohns!
- The improviser who, after taking night classes to learn to speak French, finds himself onstage when an audience member yells out the suggestion of Marie Antoinette. His campy, but "realistically French" speaking executioner is the highlight of the scene.

You need to determine what setting and environment is most conducive to your creativity and productivity. And check the tools you have and use to accomplish your work. Are they the right tools? Would a portable tape recorder suit you better at meetings than a pen and paper? How about jazzing up your office with a few cool items you just brought back from your trip to the Far East? Might they inspire great memories and unique sparks? Maybe you want to put a handwritten banner across your wall that says, *Got Sparks?*

Try a number of different things; see how they work and if they don't float your boat . . . shake it up again. Don't be complacent, don't settle, and don't try to force it. Instead, take the sage advice of Obi Wan Kenobi when he said, "Use the force, Luke . . . to ignite a spark . . . a spark that leads to spontaneous combustion." All right, all right, we added that last part, but you get the point.

TIPS ON THE TOPIC

- A spark can never be manufactured; it can only be experienced.
- Your mind should get still—be still—stay still.
- Fill the well—personal and work.
- Create the "right conditions" for combustion.

PERSONAL EXERCISE 3
Turtles Are Great!

The Players: You, an egg timer, a tape recorder, and a few unrelated props.

The Object: To create a "spontaneous combustion brainstorm" by energetically verbalizing a list of possibilities. The experience—The player must describe imaginary uses for a simple household object in a timed stream-of-consciousness rant.

How To: 1. Gather a bag full of six or seven unrelated household objects. Keep them simple. (For example: a dinner plate, a toothbrush, a candle, a spoon, a tennis racquet, and a beanie baby stuffed turtle.)

2. Let's start with the turtle, for example. Turn the egg timer to two minutes, and turn on the tape recorder.

3. It's time to be in the moment, and out of your mind. Gaze at the turtle and begin by exclaim-

ing "Turtles are great, because . . ." Then rapidly and with commitment, launch into a list of why turtles are great in any and every way except why they are actually great.

Hint:

That is, avoid "Turtles are great, because they make a fine pet" (real), or "Turtles are great because they make a hearty yet pricey soup" (real). Rather try "Turtles are great because you can tape a FedEx package to their backs and turtles will get it there—Same Year Delivery" or, "Turtles are great because you can skip them on the water like a flat rock" or, "Turtles are great because you can varnish them and use them as living bookends." Get the idea?

4. Stop talking and stop the tape after two minutes. *Rewind and listen to your list.* How many did you do? Make a note of the number, and repeat with the same object. Try to increase the number of ideas the second time around. Try to be more descriptive.

5. Keep playing this game until you think it's absolutely impossible to come up with anything else for which "turtles are great." And then let the game go on and on. And on.

6. Increase the time to three minutes.

7. Choose another object, and repeat the above until your mental muscle feels like a marshmallow.

The Result: In "Turtles Are Great!" you will stretch your ability to think on your feet with increased originality and imagination, while remaining in the moment. *Stick with this game.*

We promise you that you'll find the most insanely creative ideas appear *after* you think you've exhausted your options!

FOUR

IN THE MOMENT AND OUT OF YOUR MIND

Du400ring this chapter the following words will pop up more times than a tart.

- Focus
- Energy out
- Commitment

They are the linchpins to getting in the moment, being in the moment, and staying in the moment. If you would like some tools to help you to live in the moment while being out of your mind, you've come to the right place. But first, a moment of silence.

R.I.P.
Creativity

Repetition is responsible for the death of creativity; cold, calculated, and premeditated. When Cain (founding father of the N.R.A.—National Rock Association) picked a stone to slay his brother he made a creative choice. Maybe not a sound and rational choice, but it was new, different, and he was definitely In The Moment. And what does that mean, being in the moment? Well, in the case of Cain, it means he reacted only to the situation he was experiencing at that time (*focus*), his attentions were concentrated solely on his unwitting brother (*energy out*), and he started something, heightened it, and never stopped until he was finished (*commitment*). He reacted to the moment by simply being in the moment.

What happens when you're not in the moment? Awful, horrible things happen . . . to very good people. Take us for instance. We were running a corporate workshop on team building and creativity with being in the moment as the central theme. Things were moving along quite smoothly until a voice from the back of the room pierced the air: "Oh my God, it's a bat!" At that moment we missed a golden opportunity to sense what everyone else felt—that the focus had shifted from us to our uninvited motivational squeaker. While a few ran seeking refuge and others launched paper cups into the air, we forged on. While others covered their heads, we covered important information. Eventually our furry friend was escorted from the room and undivided attention was once again ours. But in that brief respite from normalcy, we failed to heed what was our intended message: Live in the moment. We failed to follow the most basic tenet of improvisation: Expect the unexpected. And we knew it. Of course, the remainder of the workshop was smooth sailing, but for a moment we lost our focus, turned our energy inward, and never fully committed to what was really happening. And that's all it takes—a moment. It wasn't a part of our plan and was nowhere mentioned on our index cards.

And the really scary thing? It could happen to you. It may not be a bat, but it could be a stock tumble the day before your annual stockholders' meeting. Or a thunderstorm on the day of your daughter's outdoor wedding. Or, higher power forbid, you delete all of your PowerPoint slides minutes before your presentation. Bad things may happen to good people, but they never happen to those who expect the unexpected and live in the moment.

In chapter 3 you learned to recognize the spark as you prepared to spontaneously combust. And as combustion begins, if you allow yourself to be in the moment, you will experience the following: You will react more truthfully, you'll eliminate outcome-based expectations, and you'll experience everything that is happening as new, different, and wonderful.

> Spontaneity is the moment of personal freedom when we are faced with a reality and see it, explore it and act accordingly.
> —Viola Spolin, *Improvisation for the Theater*

Repetition in the workplace is responsible for the death of corporate creativity. There are deadlines to meet, customers to greet, meetings to attend, and memos you need to send.

There are deadlines to meet, customers to greet, meetings to attend . . . you get the picture. But every so often an individual breaks rank, takes a calculated risk, and proves that those who live in the trenches, by digging a little deeper, find hidden treasures.

"I would like this . . . 'to go'!"

Following a very successful Out of the Blue workshop with the frontline staff of a prestigious resort in the Florida Keys, the three of us sat down at the resort's best restaurant to gorge on anything you could catch from a boat, other than a cold. Our mood was upbeat and playful. Our server was a young gentleman named Michael, who had not had the benefit of our workshop earlier that day. He was confident, professional, and extremely pleasant. He seemed to take in full stride the fact that we were throwing out verbal jabs at one another and mocking the credibility of one another's existence, with Molly still finding time to lob an occasional playful derision in his direction. Well, after the three of us had enjoyed a couple of glasses of wine and a multitude of crab legs, Michael broke out of his shell in a fashion that we will never forget. Upon returning to our table he simply asked, "May I remove the mess from your table?" No sooner had we mumbled an affirmative than he promptly grabbed Molly's chair, Molly aboard, and pushed it away from the table and across the room. We doubled over with laughter and Michael doubled his tip. Sure, he took a risk, but not an uncalculated one. He focused, turned his energy out, and then committed fully to his actions. He didn't go by the book. He followed his intuitions and lived in the moment.

So, what can you do right now to start living your life, both work and personal, in a manner that reflects an in-the-moment attitude? Let's start by looking at the first of our three linchpins: Focus.

HOCUS, POCUS . . . FOCUS!

Focus, like sanity, sometimes just seems to come and go. When watching an improvisation scene, even the novice viewer can spot times when the focus of the actors starts to wander. Signs? The scene loses momentum, the actors are less bold, physically and emotionally, they stop listening fully, and a nervous energy pervades the stage. That nervous energy is then transmitted to the audience, which becomes uncomfortable and eventually disconnects.

Loss of focus also happens in the real world, but with consequences that can prove much more dire: A surgeon in a Tampa, Florida, hospital amputates the wrong foot during an operation. Within months doctors fuse the wrong vertebrae together on a patient . . . at the same hospital. Eyewitness testimonies, putting hundreds of people behind bars for lengthy sentences, are proven inaccurate thanks to DNA testing.

On the flip side, sharpening focus can be life changing as well: Hypnotists bring people to calming hypnotic stages, then focus on solutions for certain problems, like quitting smoking, with great success. Every day scientists and medical laboratories get one step closer to finding treatments and hopefully cures for AIDS, Parkinson's disease, and various forms of cancer by narrowing the pinpoint focus of their studies.

In improvisation we train actors in a technique that helps them stay engaged in the moment without losing touch with their part in the scene as a whole. This method works in the business world as well. And it is important because the requirements of multitasking are not about to go away. What we can do is prioritize, and stay in the moment by using this technique.

Warning! It is imperative that you first become skilled at staying in the moment before attempting the following technique. Remember—small steps.

The Bifocal Technique

Simply put, the bifocal technique allows you to focus on each moment in the scene of your life as it is happening (dominant focus), while at the same time having a softer focus on the entire experience as it develops (peripheral focus). The following is a straightforward example of using the bifocal technique in a customer-service setting. We like to call it: "Pharmacist—Heal Thyself."

You work in a pharmacy. You are filling the prescription of a truly delightful older gentleman when without warning another customer, a man you've had difficult dealings with in prior situations, enters the drugstore and stands in your line. What should you do? Well, it is absolutely essential that you don't lose sight of your dominant focus (the delightful gentleman). As long as he is at your counter you must not let the expectation of what might happen next influence how you deal with him. Of course, you cannot and should not totally ignore the man at the back of the line. In fact, making him a part of your peripheral focus may be doing yourself a big favor. Make the first connection. Smile and assure him, as you have with all the others, that you'll be with him shortly. Then, when it's not stealing focus from your present customer, take another glance and check in with your potential difficult customer. Maybe today his mood is good and upbeat, maybe not. Look for any interactions he may have with the other customers. We can often pick up clues from watching interactions that don't include us. Remember, the others are all part of our peripheral focus. By the time this gentleman reaches the counter, you'll have already sharpened your focus and will be ready to interact in the moment. As Yogi Berra once said, "You can observe a lot by just watching."

Since experience is the key to practical application, let's add the following drill to your experiential portfolio.

YOU KNOW THE IMPROV DRILL

I Am the Camera

This is a great lunchtime activity. It works like this: Grab your lunch, grab a pen and paper, and grab a seat—alone if possible. Look down at your table and after a few seconds look up and lock focus on the first person you see and note one very specific thing about this person. Then snap that shot in your mind. Now look away from this person and lock your focus on someone or something else. Note one very specific thing and then snap that shot in your mind. Continue until you've snapped about ten shots. Now grab your pen and paper and write down the ten specific things that stood out in your mind's photos. See how many you can recall. As you continue to do this drill and your focus gets sharper, challenge yourself and shoot with a roll of brain-film that has more exposures.

The application of this drill to your work environment or even your family life is that strengthening our ability to really focus on specific moments (information) allows us to stay in the moment without fear that we will forget everything that happened prior to this moment. That is the key of the bifocal technique.

ENERGY OUT

Energy, as we know, is in a constant state of flow. And by observing other human beings, household pets, and even the mighty oceans, you can see that it varies in its level and intensity. Think of the following people and choose a word that best describes them in terms of energy. The first one is on the house.

Robin Williams	Relentless
Homer Simpson	_____
Larry King	_____
The Rock	_____
Britney Spears	_____
George W. Bush	_____

As you can see the spectrum of energy is vast and varied. But no matter how you or others would describe your level of energy, it's not what's truly important. What's most important is what you do with the energy you have and where you focus it.

Let's look at Robin Williams. One might assume that when you expend more energy you become more effective. The problem is, if your energy is random and unfocused it is of little or no value. It attacks our senses instead of connecting to them. And at the risk of alienating Mr. Williams, his need for frenetic levels of energy is more about him than it is about us. It may seem like energy focused out, but in reality, it is energy focused in. It keeps him in the focal point and demands our attention. And, we give it to him because he is funny—very funny. But think about it. How do we look at people like Robin Williams, people who operate at the same level of intensity, but who are *not* funny? Every one of us knows someone like this. And their simple presence has us looking for a back door and a cab to . . . anywhere.

IMPROVISE THIS!

How can we train ourselves to put our energy out to others in the scenes of our lives? How can we make others the focal point and give them our attention? Here are four short disciplines to help you point your energy in the right direction.

YOU KNOW THE IMPROV DRILL

Four for One and All for You

GET EMPTY

Forget about what happened yesterday. Start with a clean slate. What can make today different? Try parking your car in a different spot, throw back the front seat, and crank up your favorite CD, one that makes you feel good all over. Don't think about it; just let it wash over you. And sing out! When you're finished, enter the building from a different direction using a different door. And bring your new outlook with you; don't leave it in the parking lot. It's a brand-new day.

VISUALIZE

Before leaving the house, or in your car, the subway or the bus, close your eyes and visualize for five minutes. Imagine yourself putting out beams of positive energy that connect to the people around you. Watch that energy make them more positive and successful. So successful that you're named CEO with three months' paid vacation and stock options! Why not, it's your visualization.

WALK THE STAGE

Once in your work environment, take a few moments to walk around and take it all in. Try to see it through a new set of eyes. Visualize yourself in this environment. How can you connect more strongly to the space? Think of how you can derive positive energy from the space to feed to the people with whom you work. Walk it, know it, change it, and then change it again.

GET LOOSE

When we are relaxed we give off that energy, which makes those around us relax. Work often makes us tense. Find a few times during the day to get up, stretch out, take a brisk walk or do five situps. And don't forget your mind, it needs to get loose too. Hold a book upside down and try to read it, make a paper airplane and toss it out of your door, grab the daily newspaper and work on the crossword puzzle or the word jumble. Anything that isn't work will allow you to access a different part of your brain and have a little fun.

COMMITMENT

As we moved into the twenty-first century it was imperative that we left something behind and made room for what was to come. Unfortunately, what we left behind was our sense of patience and willingness to commit to anything for an extended period of time. Our attention spans have become much shorter and our need for constant stimulation has become alarmingly apparent. Television and the allure of advertising play a major role in our diminished capacity to focus on what we already have. We want something new and we want it now.

Improvisers suffer from an affliction directly related to this diminished capacity to focus. It's called: the Shiny Object Syndrome. Another appropriate label would be the "bad blind date syndrome." Regardless of its handle, with improvisers the symptoms are easily recognizable.

- Endlessly long pauses (not for effect)
- Over talking
- Confusion of purpose
- Lack of trust

When an unseasoned improviser experiences one of these moments, they often hear a voice, the tiny little voice of self-doubt. This little voice will quickly and repeatedly tell the improviser all sorts of horrible things like, "You have no business doing improvisation." That people see them for the charlatan that they are. That his or her mother did, in fact, wear army boots. When this happens, there is only one way to quiet the voice of self-doubt: Distract it. Give it something new to look at. A shiny object!

In terms of improvisation scenes, here's what could happen. The scene hits some sort of roadblock. In this case, there is confusion as to a character's identity. So far, two different actors in the scene have been called Marvin and now no one is quite sure what to do. Which actor really is Marvin? Instead of someone, anyone, committing to resolution ("Of course we're both named Marvin, we were once conjoined twins connected at the ankle") all of the actors in the scene abandon the difficult moment and move on, focusing on something entirely new (the shiny object). "Why look, the neighbors' barn just fell down!"

Although it's not quite so easy to arrogantly discard difficult things in the business world and just move on, it does happen. Why? It usually stems from our fear of commitment, the fear of rolling up our sleeves and getting in and getting dirty. Commitment to hard work, without guarantee of success, is a tall order. Some people thrive in this atmosphere of "let's just do it," others do not.

For those who are susceptible to the Shiny Object Syndrome, help is on the way. It starts with a simple, yet honest self-appraisal. "Do I live in the moment?" "Do I focus my energies out?" "Do I commit to anything?" Once you've taken this self-inventory you only need to do one thing. You only need to figure out the positive elements of who you are and just be more of that!—just be more of you!

By starting from a place of strength (who you already are) and committing to be more of that, you will remain in a confident state. Over time you can work on any of the other areas you feel need addressing, but for now just commit to be more of the positive things you are.

The exercise at the end of this chapter is one great method to personalize this commitment to being more of you. We use it extensively in our workshops and training. It's fun, and at the same time an excellent barometer for self-awareness.

Mental Wealth Benefits

Before moving on, take a few minutes to ponder the personal benefits you might expect from living in the moment. We like to think of it this way: Video cameras are a wonderful creation. They record the memories of our lives. We can record something and go back to watch it time and time again: Bobby's baptism, the family trip to Disney World, your wife's surprise fortieth birthday party, your surprise fiftieth birthday party (paybacks are hell). There is just one problem: These memories are recorded through the eye of the camera, which is incapable of emotion. This means that if you were the one filming at the moment these events occurred, you were one step removed from the actual event. You saw it, you heard it, you were in the middle of it, but you weren't 100 percent available to experience it. Your experience was compromised by having to operate the camera—focus, press, zoom, etc.

Our recommendation? The next time you go to your son's or daughter's soccer game, bring a folding chair, set it up in a good spot and watch—intently. Listen, observe, experience. You will create a memory that lasts longer than any videotape, and the emotional satisfaction of giving 100 percent of yourself to the moment will make the experience that much richer. In addition, when your child asks, "Did you see when I kicked the ball and it hit the pipe?" you can look him or her straight in the eye and say "Yes . . . And!"

TIPS ON THE TOPIC

- Sharpen your focus by refusing to clutter it with expectations and becoming results-oriented.
- Look for and listen for specifics. Give specifics in return.
- Trust in the bifocal technique. Incorporating dominant and peripheral focus can work when you're truly in the moment.
- Focus energy out to others instead of in on ourselves.
- Commit to the moment. Don't be led astray by the shiny object.

PERSONAL EXERCISE 4
Personal Energy—Your "Theme Song"

You may not be aware of it, but you have your own personal theme song. And just like Dick Van Dyke's, it plays every time you walk into a room. Hopefully, it doesn't start with *dum dum, dum dum,* as in the theme from *Jaws,* but it might. Or it might be the theme from *Survivor* (the band or the show!). It could be the theme from *Sesame Street.* As important as knowing the name of your own theme song (personal energy) is simply knowing that you have one and that it is consistent with the energy you believe you give off to others. If you walk into a room and everyone hears the music from the shower scene in *Psycho* and you're thinking the theme from *Love Story,* well . . . Houston, we've got a problem!

The Players: You and your acquaintances.

The Object: To discover the name(s) of your own personal "theme song(s)"—which is a useful analogy for the positive or negative energy that you give off to others daily.

How To: A fine way to discover the name of your theme song is to start by asking yourself. Then ask people you trust. Ask a family member, a colleague, or someone from your social circle. Kids are great because they tend to be direct. Also, pay close attention to how people react when you enter a room.

Is the reaction consistent over time? Is it consistent with the energy you want to give off?

Name your theme song or songs. Be honest with yourself. (But not overly serious, please.) Write them down, along with who suggested them, in your improv journal. Are they inspiring and energetic tunes such as "Climb Every Mountain" or the depressed "Eeyore's Lament"? Are they somewhere in between?

Now, if need be, choose another—your ideal theme song. Make it positive, up-tempo, and personal.

When you get a good sense of the energy you want to put out as symbolized by your new song, then every day try to just be more of that. Be more of the guy whose theme song is "Don't Worry, Be Happy." Be more of the woman whose theme song is "Rocky." Whatever you choose as your ideal personal theme song, commit, live it, and be more of it.

The Result: We use this game often in our playshops and training. It's an excellent barometer for self-awareness. The result is a sensitized perspective on how you see yourself, and how others see you in terms of the positive or negative energy you put out to the world around you.

The Authors' Own Very Personal Theme Songs

Mark: In my best moments I certainly like to think my theme song is Van (the Man) Morrison's "Moondance." A little cool and moody sometimes, but with an undercurrent of upbeat energy and good feeling. (Note: This personal theme song also reflects the revealing nickname my high school girlfriend gave me those many years ago when I gloomily shuffled into some long-forgotten lunchroom: "Oh boy. Here comes 'Mark the Dark.'" I've been working on it, I swear.)

Molly: As a woman of many moods (almost all good) and attitudes, narrowing it down is a difficult task. But, I believe that the essence of my spirit and the energy that sweeps into the room even before I do would probably be captured in the Aretha Franklin R & B classic "R-E-S-P-E-C-T." Although both of my partners contend that a more apt selection would be Cher's "Gypsies, Tramps and Thieves." I don't always like my business partners.

Jim: I'd have to say that I have two quite different theme songs that come to mind for myself. The first is the seventies disco hit—"I Will Survive." Mainly because I have the feeling that people sense that no matter where we may go (during a meeting, training, etc.), I'll get them back safely, and hopefully on time. The second is a song by the group Barenaked Ladies called "Grade 9." This song is a high-energy ode to being a semi-geek ninth grader. It's a self-image fear that I have successfully stuffed so deep that no therapist could ever find it. It's actually hidden just behind my spleen.

FAMOUS PEOPLE WHO SHOULD HAVE IMPROVISED . . .
AND WHAT THEY COULD HAVE SAID

Time out for a tongue-in-cheek satirical take on a few celebrities and political figures who were caught like the proverbial deer in the headlights during awkward situations on the national or international stage. We've all seen it happen. And squirmed right along with the poor idiots. Let's theorize, shall we, on what they could have said if they were (of course) well versed in our improvisation techniques and could think on their feet, instead of having a serious case of foot-in-mouth.

Hail to the Chief?

Early in his presidential campaign, then-candidate George W. Bush was ambushed by Andy Hiller, a TV reporter from WHDH, Boston, and given the infamous "pop quiz." Cameras rolling, the reporter (obviously a flaming liberal and another "ass____, big time") asked candidate GW to "name the leaders of Taiwan, Chechnya, Pakistan, and India." Governor Bush named (correctly) "Lee" as the leader of Taiwan, but then froze. Obviously flummoxed, he fumbled the rest of his response and failed miserably.

What he said: "What is this . . . 50 questions?"*

What he could have said:

"Hmm. [Pause for effect] Great question. But on second thought Bob, I'll take 'Chinese Fund-raisers' for a hundred, please . . ."

*Source: *The Boston Globe.*

To Tell You the Truth . . .

O. J. Simpson, football star, movie star, and star witness, apparently had trouble thinking on his feet during his sworn deposition at the civil trial. When questioned on his whereabouts at the time of the crime:

> What he said: He testified that he was "chipping golf balls in his yard" (at ten o'clock *at night*) and then went upstairs. "I was kind of spacing," he said. "I had a book in my lap and my TV was on, so I was just sort of spacing."*

Now we're not saying that he wasn't telling the truth. Not at all. However, this is

> What he could have said:
>
> "Where was I? Easy! Kato and I were in my yard playing our usual Thursday night game of 'hide the bloody glove' and time just sort of got away from me . . ."

It's All in How You Look at It . . .

Bill Clinton. What he said: "I did not have sexual relations with that woman."

What he could have said: "Did I have sexual relations with that woman? Hmmm. Define 'I'—"

---

*Source: CNN Web Site—O.J. Simpson. "Simpson Deposition Transcripts Released." Posted March 5, 1996.

AN INSIDE TIP FROM OUTSIDE THE BOX

MO COLLINS
Improvisational Actor

Mo Collins grew up in the twin cities of Minneapolis and St. Paul. Mo cut her comedy teeth as a member of both the touring and resident companies of Dudley Riggs's Brave New Workshop, in Minneapolis. A veteran stage performer and truly gifted comedian, she is now in her fourth season of Fox's *MAD TV,* where she has created a cadre of memorable characters. Mo, her husband, Jim, and their six-year-old son, Cullen, reside in North Hollywood, California.

Q: Do you remember your first formal introduction to improvisation?

A: *Yes, definitely. It was in eighth grade thanks to a wonderful teacher named Ertwin Marvin Jones-Hermerding, a.k.a. "Ert" and "Herm." We used improvisation to write sketch shows, which we performed, for our junior high as well as some of the local high schools. Everything that we did was original. It was an unbelievable experience that shaped my life. I'm forever in debt to Herm for introducing me to one of the great loves of my life—improv.*

Q: So, was he your first improvisation role model?

A: *Actually, no. That would be my mother.*

Q: How so?

A: *Well. When there was nothing in the kitchen, she'd improvise a completely original meal out of nothing . . . and make it fun.*

Q: So, is improv now "a way of life" for you or do you just use it in one or two areas?

A: *It's a way of life. I'm not disciplined enough to plan ahead. As much as possible I try to go with my first gut instinct on things. Sometimes this is referred to as "fools rush in." (Laughter)*

Q. Well, it's okay. This interview is "foolproof." (Laughter stops) Sorry. Moving on . . . Mo, what is your definition of improvisation?

A: *Creative freedom and creative relief—therapy. If I'm having a bad day, when I get on stage and do improvisation, I'm able to escape my own troubles and be somebody else for a bit. It can often turn a day around. Give you the mental boost you couldn't otherwise find that day.*

Q. Therapy? Sounds good. Any other benefits you see from doing improv?

A: *Health, dental and life? Yeah, plenty . . . it can help you to be a more flexible person in the world. It helps you roll with the punches. Be a risk taker! (Mo got extremely loud at this point.)*

Q. What impact does improvising have on your personal life?

A: *It has allowed me to be something more than what I originally thought of myself. I grew up very shy and improv helped me to see that I'm somebody more than that. I think it can also help you to understand other people—*

Q. (Interrupting) In what way?

A: *When you're doing character work and you step into the shoes of another person you can experience things you may not know yourself. You learn to empathize . . . It teaches you to have compassion for others. And it allows you to react off other people in ways you may not normally do in real life. And, it simply keeps me from going insane. Without it, I do believe my head would explode.*

Q: Okay, before that happens . . . your personal life . . . you have a six-year-old son. What goes on there, in regard to improvisation?

A: *I'm flying by the seat of my pants all the time with Cullen. Playtime, mealtime, it's great. My greatest joy is getting to teach him the ideals of improvisation. Not that we stand around doing "spots" or "heralds" [improv games]. I do my best to teach him that we are all equal on the playing field. It's teamwork. It's sometimes letting go of preconceived notions about how things were supposed to go and finding joy or peace or reason in the new result. For example, who said a Power Ranger is any less powerful without a leg?*

Q. So, you promote Cullen's use of improvisation to help him become anything he sets his mind to and follow whatever his heart desires?

A: *Yep, as long as it doesn't involve candy, motorcycles, or Zima.*

Q: Since this book is primarily for business folk, let us ask. Are there any businesses that you have dealt with that seem to embody the principles of improvisation?

A: *Businesses don't come to mind, but individuals within their businesses, yes. I would say some banks could start implementing the ideals of improv. Businesses tend to think their power is in rigidity and rules and "this it how it's always been done." There is power in letting go. Taking risks. That is where the greatest rewards are. Improvising is a terrific risk, because you don't yet know how or where it's going to end.*

What a wonderful thing. There is disappointment when you plan to such a degree and things don't go your way. There is great surprise when you allow room for grace to step in—faith!

Q: Any advice for someone who is just getting started in improvisation?

A: *Sure, just let go. Trust yourself and others. Trust your scene partner. And never limit your creative self.*

Q: What about the fear factor?

A: *It can, no, will, be scary, but you've just gotta gear up for it. As for failing, there is no failing, because improv rules aren't written in stone. There are no improv police—as of yet.*

Q: Okay, one final question. Can you describe the internal feeling you get when you are in improvisation mode?

A: *It feels giddy and empowering. Sometimes my stomach makes me sick—of course, that could just be gas.*

FIVE

ACTIVE LISTENING

You Can't Hear the Sea When You're Inside the Shell

The reason you don't understand me, Edith, is 'cause I'm
talkin' to you in English and you're listening to me in Dingbat!
—Archie Bunker

Improvisation classes spend a great deal of time teaching listening. And the most successful students are the ones who
understand and embrace the concept that listening, actively
listening, is one of the most important skills—some call it an
art—they can master. Since they have no idea what they or
their scene partner or partners are about to say, and the success of the scene hinges on sharing information and building
a scene from that, improvisers can't afford to miss *any* information.

Unfortunately, most improvisers are not very good listeners. Actually, the same can be said for people in the business world. And people in relationships. Let's face it, not many of us can lay claim to being really good listeners. Interestingly enough, in the corporate world, where decisions involving thousands of people and millions of dollars are made every day, you really needn't be more than a marginally good listener to be successful . . . at least in the short term. The same can be said for partners in a relationship . . . in the short term. But show us an improviser who isn't a splendid listener and we'll show you an improviser who can bring any scene down like a house of cards.

Here's a simple way to look at the importance of listening:

Active listening leads to better communication, which leads to stronger relationships, and stronger relationships are the anchor of any good improv scene or successful business.

So, listen up and we'll show you ways to assess your listening prowess, to improve your ability to be a better listener, to break bad non-listening habits, and to make communication (and therefore any relationship) easier.

But before we get started, let's take a moment and learn some interesting statistics about listening and communication.

Have You Heard?

- Amount of time we are distracted, preoccupied, or forgetful: 75%
- How much we usually recall immediately after we listen to someone talk: 50%

- Amount of time we spend listening to others: 45%
- How much we remember of what we hear: 20%
- We listen at 125–250 words per minute, but we think at 1,000–3,000 words per minute.
- Number of business studies that indicate that listening is a top skill needed for success in business? More than 35!
- Amount of us who have had formal educational experience with listening: 2%★

ARE YOU TALKIN' TO ME?

The best way to understand people is to listen to them. But it's a lot of work to listen. To really listen takes concentration, commitment, and interest. And it takes practice to learn how to do it well. So let's practice. If you aren't sure where you fall in the category of listening skills, here's a quick exercise for you: *Ask people.* Yep, just start asking people if they think you're a good listener or not. It is best not to start with your spouse or partner—especially if you're pretty darn sure what the answer is going to be. So, start with someone safe. Someone you trust. Yes, your dog *is* a safe bet, but we're asking you to dig deeper. Ask someone who will give you *honest* feedback, like your cat.

YOU KNOW THE IMPROV DRILL

Listen Up!

Ask a friend or coworker if they have a few minutes to talk with you. Find a quiet place where you can give your undivided attention to the other person.

★Source: High Gain, Inc.

1. Tell them that you want to find out more about yourself. You want to build your good qualities and improve on others.
2. Ask them to assess your listening skills. Ask if they think you are a good listener. Are there areas you could improve? Be quiet while they answer you. It may take some time for them to form an answer. That's okay. Give them time. Be patient and wait. Don't prompt them in any way. Give them your full physical attention. Don't interrupt or direct their answers.
3. Do this with several people, each time quietly listening to what they say about you. You might not like what you hear. Or you may be pleasantly surprised. Either way, you'll learn something about yourself. Pearl Bailey once said, "To talk to someone who does not listen is enough to tense the devil." We think a good rule of thumb is to stay on the devil's good side. Of course, the devil probably doesn't have a good side, so this rule of thumb may have to be considered more fully at a future time.

Having a clear sense of how others perceive your listening skill level is a wonderful place to start. And now it's time to spin the mirror around and make a few honest self-observations. We want you to think about what happens when you interact with someone.

What is it that you do when you are listening to someone, anyone—a sibling, parent, coworker, friend, or the guy who plops down next to you on the bus? What are your habits? Do you fiddle with "stuff"? Do you type on the computer when you're on the phone? (How irritating is it to hear that *clicking* when you're talking with someone?) Do you look the person straight in the eye? Do you give feedback to the speaker, letting him know you're listening—"oh," "yes," "really?" What is your body doing during these conversations? Do you interrupt? Do you listen without judgment? Take a few minutes to really think about it. Jot your answers down in your journal. What is it you do when you're supposed to be listening?

WHY YOU CANNOT *NOT* COMMUNICATE

People have been communicating in one form or another since 500,000,567 B.C. Or, in any case, for a very long time. And a lot of that communication was just plain ol' grunting, body language, and some pulling of the hair. It was not often that the average caveman broke away from spearing dinner to attend a seminar on communication skills. Although we're sure improvisation was *huge,* as evidenced by the early cave drawings for the show *Whose Cave Is It Anyway?* No matter how primitive, you cannot *not* communicate.

Listening requires the use of your body, not just your ears, but your *entire* body. It requires being in the moment and paying attention. If communication is broken down into three categories, as the experts tell us—nonverbal 55 percent, the actual *words* we use only 7 percent, but the *tone* of those words 38 percent—then heads up; there's a lot to learn here. This chapter may help you move up the corporate ladder *and* save your marriage. Both are worth learning this skill (provided you like the company you work for and your spouse).

BODY LANGUAGE

Let's start with body language. At the risk of receiving letters from NOW, we're going to offer a classic female scenario. Most females are born with an innate skill to communicate what they are thinking without words. It is called "the Look," and men fear it across all racial and economic planes. It goes like this:

Setting: Man and woman attending dinner party at the woman's boss's home.

WOMAN: What great work on the Zippo account, sir. You had them wrapped around your finger in the first two minutes!

MAN: Honey, are you kidding? You just said the presentation on the Zippo Account bomb—

WOMAN: [Gives THE LOOK. Translation: "Shut up right now before I shove this dinner roll up your nose."]

Now, that's just one example. You would have to have been raised on a desert island with no females to have not experienced "the Look." We need not go on. Let's just say this is a good example of the 55 percent part of the communication rule. Moral: You can avoid getting a roll shoved up your nose if you are able to interpret body language clues.

I "See" What You're Saying

Body language is the unspoken communication that goes on in every face-to-face encounter. It screams out someone's true feelings and expresses the meaning behind the words. Consider flirting. What if we had to rely solely on words to flirt with someone? There would be a lawsuit extravaganza. It just wouldn't work. And it certainly wouldn't be much fun. Flirting is based on a range of courtship "signals." Some are blatant and deliberate; some are completely unconscious. In an improvised scene, the audience can be completely mesmerized by a silent scene between two people flirting. Researchers agree that generally the verbal channel is used primarily to convey information, while the nonverbal is used for negotiating interpersonal attitudes. Watching people flirt is a great way to study body language and interpersonal communication signals. Watching them too closely is a great way to get a restraining order.

Me, Myself, and Eye

"Eyes are the window to the soul," "There was so much love in his eyes," "If looks could kill," "Her eyes glazed over." We constantly communicate with our eyes, so it's important to be aware of the messages we're sending out, as well as to be able to read what messages others are sending us. Eyes are an amazing indicator of interest and can send signals that a person is anywhere from riveted to comatose (any presenter, present company excluded, has experienced both). Any competent salesperson will be able to tell if a prospect is "with them" by focusing on their eye language. Why? Because the eyes speak volumes.

In improvisation, eye contact is imperative, because, as in life, there is no script telling us who is supposed to speak next. And eye contact doesn't necessarily mean eye-to-eye contact. It more often means eye-to-whomever you're interacting with at the moment and what they're doing contact. The finest improvisers are excellent observers. They can pick up the smallest detail, the slightest minutia, by keeping their communication antennae up at all times.

There is a saying, "Your actions speak so loudly I can't hear what you're saying." From this moment forward, pay attention to how you stand when you're told something you don't want to hear. Are your arms crossed at your chest? Do you stand with your feet apart in a defensive position? Do your eyes focus on anything but the person you're, dare we say, communicating with? Trust that they, using their eyes to listen, are hearing this message loud and clear: "I don't like the information coming my way . . . I'm not going to be open to it." The opposite holds true when we are receiving information we like. We have open arms and our facial muscles are relaxed. You may not even be aware of what you're doing. Negative body language puts up barriers between us and the person who's talking. If your fists are clenched and you're punching a pillow as someone talks to you, you already know what message you're sending. And you should probably check out a community anger management course.

As you start to become more aware of how you communicate, pay attention to the way others take in information. We mentioned gender earlier; there are also typical communication patterns within age groups.

Has this ever happened to you? Watch what a thirteen-year-old girl does when you tell her to fold the laundry. You may hear what she does first. "That is, like, so not fair." But what you will generally see is her eyes roll around, à la Linda Blair, and a huge sigh will be released into the atmosphere. No words needed. Forty-five minutes later, when the laundry still hasn't been folded, she will say, "You never told me to do that." That is the difference between listening and hearing.

In her book *Listening, the Forgotten Skill,* author Madelyn Burley-Allen points out that most people are only 25 percent effective as listeners, and they don't even realize how poor their skills are. However, as teenagers cannot be classified as "people," they don't fall into the 25 percent rule.

HOW DO I LEARN TO REALLY LISTEN TO THE WORDS SOMEONE IS SAYING?

> An essential part of true listening is the discipline of bracketing,
> the temporary giving up or setting aside of one's own
> prejudices, frames of reference and desires so as to
> experience as far as possible the speaker's world from the
> inside, step inside his shoes . . . as this happens, speaker
> and listener appreciate each other more.
> —M. Scott Peck, *The Road Less Traveled*

If you really want to become a better listener and therefore a better communicator, there are a few simple practices that you can employ to help you reach your goal.

- *Never interrupt.* There is nothing so important that it can't keep until your communication partner is finished speaking.
- *Listen without judgment.* The second you begin to break down and judge what is being said to you is the exact same second you stop listening. Remain objective.
- *Be Clear—Be Concise.* One excellent way to heighten your own ability to listen is to help your life scene partner by being more specific when you speak. By carefully choosing thoughts and painting your dialogue with words that best describe your feelings or thoughts, instead of more general words or terms, you not only help your scene partner gain understanding, you also strengthen your own ability to listen for and detect specific words and intentions when you communicate. Example: (general) It was a very nice fall day. (concise) It was a crystal-blue-sky, leaf-pile-jumping, crisp autumn day.

- *If you don't know, ask!* Never be afraid to ask for clarification when communicating. If you're not sure what you're hearing is the intended message, then by all means ask. You'll be doing both parties a favor.

Shut Up!

When teaching sales training we give out Post-It notes that simply say, "Shut Up." Then we ask people to put the notes on their phones or computers for several weeks after our program as a gentle reminder that it is the customer who should be doing the majority of the talking. The salesperson should be *listening*. It started as a joke for a major company where managers complained that their salespeople talked too much, and it ended up becoming a fun training tool and reminder to salespeople about the importance of slowing down and listening. In sales you must sell to a customer's needs, and that only happens through clear communication. You must listen not only for specific needs but also for future opportunities.

A Thought!

Wouldn't it be great if we could develop a talking "patch" for those people who talk incessantly so the withdrawal period wouldn't be so painful?

Men and Women Operate on Different Frequencies

It's only fair to spend at least a moment on the differences between the way men and women communicate. It has been said (we know this because we were listening) that women speak at least 25 percent more than men do. As Erma Bombeck once said, "A married man says about six words a night . . . and those words are not necessarily strung together to form a sentence." If this isn't enough of a difference between the sexes, consider all the new studies about the way that men listen. Turns out that men listen with only half of their brains. We will now take the upper ground and leave that alone. We just thought you should know.

Here are a few differences researchers have found when watching the different sexes communicate with each other. Women have a tendency to nod "yes," not to show they are in agreement but to show they are listening. Men, being solution-oriented, want the bottom line first, and then the details. Women tend to give the details and then the bottom line. If you want to see a very funny theatrical version of the differences between the way men and women communicate, see the Broadway play *Defending the Caveman*. Or just stop by our office sometime and watch it in action.

There have been hundreds of articles and at least three major television documentaries recently about the differences in men's and women's communication styles. The good news is that neither sex was born with innate listening skills. Great listeners and communicators work on improving this skill throughout their lives. Just for fun, become Linda Tripp or the CIA some afternoon and eavesdrop on men and women when they are talking by the water cooler, discussing a business deal, or trying to figure out their relationship. You'll pick up a lot.

Heightened Awareness

Becoming aware of your listening style and the listening styles of others in the scenes of your life helps you to communicate without feeling hurt or feeling that you aren't being heard. It will help you to improve communication and create stronger relationships. As you pay attention to the listening styles of others, remember that studies show that poor listeners are viewed as self-centered, disinterested, preoccupied, and rude! If you come in contact with them, call the local authorities, or casually slip this book on their desk. *Wait*—buy another one and slip that one on their desk. Keep this one for yourself.

Because It Feels Good

Whether it be at work or at home or with friends, having one person, just one person really listen to us, someone who is truly understanding and takes the trouble to consider our problems, can change the way we feel and our outlook on our worries.

- Are you that person for someone in your life?
- Can you be?
- What would happen if you made some small improvements in the way you listen?

One thing that could happen is you could be deeply changed by the experience. When you are able to give something of yourself to another person, you cannot help but be affected by the experience. So as you read this book and consider the information we offer, remember, it is in the doing, the experience, that change takes place. So don't think for a minute you're going to read this book, understand listening better, and . . . *poof!* you'll be loved by all and suddenly understand everything Deepak Chopra ever wrote.

You must *practice*. Improved skills may not transfer to improved listening. You must apply these skills and discipline yourself to use them in every conversation. An improviser thinks about connecting with his fellow actors before every scene. You can think about your connections and your listening acumen every day, before every interaction. Combining the desire and the practice will result in improved listening. Both you and the people you listen to will win; you'll gain an understanding of what is truly being said. Now that you're on a roll with this concept, let's review to make sure you can keep this up.

TIPS ON THE TOPIC

- Focus your undivided attention on the speaker.
- Listen with your whole body. Watch for clues.
- Keep your observation antennae up at all times.
- Let the person finish. Don't interrupt.
- Ask for clarity.
- Choose your words wisely.
- Do the exercises in this book.

Thank you for listening.

PERSONAL EXERCISE 5
Just Zip It and Listen!

The Players: You—and the person that'll be talking at you.

The Object: We are given dozens of opportunities to listen every day. When people speak to us, many times (admit it) we are half-listening and simultaneously half-scriptwriting our answers or response. This exercise depends on your complete attention and focus.

The object is to "actively listen." Laser beam focus on the speaker.

How To: "Just Zip It and Listen" can be done at home with family, at your next meeting, or anywhere you have the chance to listen to another person.

1. Turn your body to fully face the speaker. Oftentimes we think we are paying attention, but our body looks like it's late for a flight and needs to catch a cab to the airport.

2. Look into the eyes of the speaker. Throughout the conversation. (Okay, don't stare . . .)

3. With your peripheral vision, be aware of the speaker's body language, tone of voice, and speed of speech. What are they really trying to say?

4. Stop yourself from judging or jumping ahead. Or interrupting! Be in the moment.

5. Repeat this with everyone you meet. Until it becomes second nature.

The Result: Spontaneous opportunities for personal interaction are often lost simply because we don't really listen for them. People often give us "gifts" we never hear. They tell us truths we have ignored because we haven't actively listened.

The result of "Zip It and Listen" will be a fine-tuned personal communication skill—and a better intuitive understanding of what your friends, family, and coworkers are really trying to say.

SIX

"YES . . . AND!"

What You Don't "No" Won't Hurt You

Tell him to live by yes and no, yes to everything good,
no to everything bad.

—William James

We like to think of the phrase "Yes . . . And!" as the affirm
handshake that helps you get a good grip on improvisation.
You see there was a time (long before lawyers, loan officers,
and crossing your fingers behind your back) when a simple
handshake was enough. It was a strong, but silent, "Yes." It
signaled that both parties had reached an agreement and a
sense of closure. One of the most basic and vitally important
tenets of improvisation is rooted in this ancient ritual of agreement. But where a handshake in life may indicate affirmative

closure, in improvisation "Yes . . . And!" is where everything truly begins.

In order for any improviser to reach his or her maximum potential, he or she must decide to accept and adhere to the philosophy of "Yes . . . And!" Then, the task at hand becomes only slightly less challenging. In improvisational scene work, a "Yes . . . And!" improviser must still battle his or her arch-enemy—the improviser who uses the power of "No" to stop momentum, challenge trust, and close the door to discovery. Here is a quick, classic example:

IMPROVISER 1: (Entering scene) Hey, Mom, can I go to the park with Billy?
IMPROVISER 2: No, and I'm not your mother!

Our second improviser not only closed the door to discovery, she slammed it shut and engaged the deadbolt. And although the scenario may vary, little momentum-stopping scenes like this take place in the business world and the scenes of your life everyday. And, in one way or another, they involve you!

Mix and Match

Read the following question. Match each answer in column 1 to the word from column 2 that most closely resembles that answer.

"Excuse me, I've been waiting for three weeks for my Run Fast for a Short Distance cell phone to arrive. You promised me I would have it two weeks ago. Can you help me with this problem?"

"Yes . . . And!"

(1)	(2)
I don't have that information.	No!
I'm not sure why they sent you here.	No!
That's not my department.	No!
You'll have to contact my supervisor.	No!
Are you sure you didn't receive it?	No!

Our little mix and match brainteaser was based on a true story. The names were changed to protect . . . our existing service. Each answer from column one was actually said by a representative of "almost said" company during a one-week period.

NO! COMPANIES

We call companies such as the one illuminated above No! Companies. One can achieve this undesirable status in a variety of ways and for different reasons. Here are just a few:

- Rigid, inflexible policies
- Improper training of employees
- Failure to empower employees
- Consistent failure to meet customer expectations
- Poor internal communication leading to poor service
- Failure to understand the power of "Yes . . . And!"

You may work for (or run) a No! company. If so, all is not lost. There are ways to change the attitudes and practices of such environments. And all hope starts with you. So, to get a better understanding of what power you may have to bring about positive corporate culture change you need to be familiar with the things that zap your power and present the kind of monumental obstacles that would make a Marine cry.

The Ugly Stepsisters

The word "no" is extremely powerful. In many ways it's more powerful than "yes." "No" has the ability to halt forward movement, question integrity, and dismantle trust. Show us any team that operates from a place of *no* and we'll show you a team destined for mediocrity. Part of the reason for no's strength is its powerful friends who have the uncanny ability to slip into our thoughts and out of our mouths during meetings, dinners, Q&As, and blind dates. They are no's ugly stepsisters and their mere presence signals imminent doom. Their names: **Yes, but . . .** and **Yes, or . . .**

Yes, but . . . The more obvious and slightly more popular of the two, Yes, but . . . attempts to give the illusion of being affirming, yet the attempt is halfhearted at best. It often gets our hopes up just in time to dash them on the rocks. Those who use it are sometimes being sincere and sometimes just wanting the appearance of such. Here are just a few examples of Yes, but . . . in action:

QUESTION: Tom, do you like my haircut?

ANSWER: *Yes, but* it's pretty short in the back.

QUESTION: Nancy, I'm thinking about making Gail treasurer. Does that work for you?

ANSWER: *Yes, but,* Steve, she's only been with the firm for eight months.

QUESTION: Jake, would you like to come over Sunday? We're having a veal barbeque.

ANSWER: *Yes, but* I'm going to an animal rights rally, so
thanks anyway.

Let's take a closer look at our second example from above.
Nancy's response to Steve's question started with Yes, but . . .
So, what did she mean? What was her intention? Well, it's hard
to say. We're not really sure, but here are some options:

· No, I don't like her, so I'll use her short time with us as the
reason.
· No, I don't think so. She's only been here eight months. It
wouldn't be fair to her.
· Yes, but others will have problems with the choice, especially
my best friend in the company, Monica.
· Yes, but I want the position.

As you can see, Nancy's response leaves way too much room
for interpretation and Steve most likely felt Nancy's answer to
be somewhat passive aggressive. Although he put his feelings
out there and asked for Nancy's opinion, she chose to be eva-
sive—putting the onus back on Steve to figure out what she
really felt. That is the inherent problem of Yes, but: It tries to
serve two masters (yes and no) ands ends up serving neither.

The use of Yes, but . . . runs rampant—at home, at work,
even with our children. And we are all guilty of doing it on occasion. As we move through this chapter we'll show you ways
to not only heighten awareness of when we and those around
us put Yes, but . . . into play, we'll give you the tools to replace
it altogether.

When faced with the choice to say, "Yes . . . And!" or "Yes,
but . . ." the choice is clear. Use "Yes . . . And!" to keep the
exploration process alive, enhance communication, and

move closer to a positive resolution. One that can satisfy all parties involved.

As part of keeping our exploration process alive, let's check in on our other ugly stepsister.

Yes, or . . . Somewhere along the line someone got hip. They realized that people were beginning to see through their thinly veiled attempts to pass off Yes, but . . . as a positive and affirming statement. Out of their continuing need to be negative and have their own way, without appearing to be the chronic naysayer, came the phrase, Yes, or . . . Whereas Yes, but . . . offers nothing except the impending reason why something shouldn't be done, or said, or even considered, Yes, or . . . at least offers an alternative. The problem is, it still negates or at least diminishes whatever the initial offer was. Witness:

QUESTION: Dave, would you like to grab a bite to eat?

ANSWER: *Yes, or we could catch the seven o'clock movie and eat later.*

QUESTION: Mary, could you give me a lift to work tomorrow?

ANSWER: *Yes, or Doug might be able to; he lives just five minutes from you.*

On first glance Yes, or . . . seems to be wholly supportive and helpful in seeking out alternatives for the benefit of everyone. But upon further examination it becomes obvious that the responses are quite self-serving and once again, passive aggressive—attempting to manipulate a desired outcome.

It's Not Okay . . .

As you continue to build momentum toward becoming a fully realized "Yes . . . And!" person, there is something you need be aware of. There is a slight but perceptible difference between saying the word "yes" and the saying the words "okay," "yeah," "all right," "sure" and "uh huh." The difference?

The word "yes" is unmistakable in its meaning and intention. Yes means yes. The same cannot be said about the others. Although they aren't no, they aren't necessarily yes either. They sound like yes and they may be intended to be yes—they just aren't 100 percent committed, the way yes is. Think about it. Think of a time when you asked a favor of a friend, family member, or colleague. If they responded with yes, case closed. If they chose one of the other aforementioned words, you may have been left a little uncertain about their true desire to help. In that case, you may have asked the typical follow-up, "Are you sure?" Even then the answer might be, "Yeah, why not?" or "Hey, no problem!" Seldom is the response, "Yes, I'm sure." If this sounds all too familiar it's probably because you've been on the other side of the equation as well. Relax, we all have.

As we begin to check out and clear out our personal negative responses and supplant them with the highly engaging and positively inspiring "Yes!" we must be mindful that simply saying yes is not enough. Nope, we are headed for the Holy Grail of Improvisation—"Yes . . . And!" Granted, "yes" is a great start. It sets the stage for better communication, deeper exploration of ideas and makes us feel more inclusive than a nondenominational church. And we now have a much better understanding of how the word "no" abruptly halts forward movement and destroys integrity, trust, and teamwork. So, what's the secret to the success of "Yes . . . And!"?

I Got a New Attitude!

Begin by asking yourself this simple question: Am I a "yes" person? Now please, be aware that this is a completely different question than, Am I a yes-man? Not only because the term "yes-man" is exclusive in nature, assuming that it is impossible to be a yes-woman, but also because history has dictated that to be a yes-man you cannot have an opinion of your own or the ability to stand up for what you believe, that you must ride the philosophical coattails of your superiors and never question authority; in other words, to be of little or no value to yourself or your organization.

No, our question runs much deeper. It goes to the very fiber of our beings and is reflected in our approach to everything that we do. It is about an attitude, one that we ourselves get to choose. And, we get to choose it over and over, time and again each day. Am I a "Yes" person?

Think back to chapter 2 and our Five Small Steps Lead to Great Leaps. We asked you to write down one positive thing you are really good at and then say "Yes" to yourself. Did you do it? If so, there are at least two things you are really good at, one of them being a motivated self-starter. If not, here's your chance.

For the sake of argument, let's say you determine yourself to be a "Yes" person. Which means you see the glass as not only half full, but as half full of expensive champagne. You are by all assessments a normal, balanced individual with a pretty darn positive outlook on life. You enjoy challenges and stand up for what you believe, while at the same time allowing those around you to express their opinions without tuning them out or trying to force your opinion down their throats. You believe that hard work will pay off in the long run and that the system for counting votes in the United States is bound to get better, even in Florida. In short, you are a "Yes" person. Which begs the next question: Am I a "Yes . . . And!" person?

Let's say, once again, for the sake of argument, that you are indeed a "Yes . . . And!" person. You see things in a positive fashion personally and you look for the positive in others. You verbally support the contributions of your team, your friends, and your family. At work, you more than likely adopt the offerings of your colleagues, men and women equally. You adapt your contributions to build on what has already been established instead of attempting to forge your own path. You are determined to be outstanding rather than to stand out!

Unfortunately, in the business world you are still part of a large minority. And although you may have wonderful things to contribute, your voice is seldom heard over the din of that single phrase that can make a train of thought take a dirt road. It is corporate America's most complete negative catchall phrase, "We've already tried that. It won't work." Which, in an effort to conserve time and increase animosity, has been shortened to "Been there, done that!"

EXAMPLE 1

EMPLOYEE: Hey boss, I had a thought about a way to save the Baxter account. How about I schedule a conference call with them for Friday? We'll pitch adding Johnson to the project to map out Internet marketing strategies, which would allow them to move up the rollout date, so they can pass all their costs through this year's budget, giving them a huge tax break.

MR. DAVIS: No, I don't think so, Michaels. Our last conference call with Baxter was a fiasco. Besides, adding more people to the project is what killed the Meyers account. Let's just stay the course and hope for some divine intervention.

Wow, two "Been there, done thats" for the price of one.

Now, let's be very clear here. We are not for a moment suggesting that Mr. Davis should say "Yes" to something that he truly feels would be counterproductive to the situation (yes-man mentality). However, we are saying that he should say, "Yes . . . And!" to his employee's effort and look for any positive aspects of this proposal that may be worthy of further consideration. Would moving up the rollout date give Baxter a year-end tax break and save the account? Would the addition of Johnson to the team be a smart move? And what about that conference call?

Let's take one more look at this scenario with the idea that our boss, Mr. Davis, is driven by a "Yes . . . And!" philosophy.

EXAMPLE 2

EMPLOYEE: Hey boss, I had a thought about how to save the Baxter account. How about I schedule a conference call with them for Friday? We'll pitch adding Johnson to the project to map out Internet marketing strategies, which would allow them to move up the rollout date, so they can pass all their costs through this year's budget, giving them a huge tax break.

MR. DAVIS: Well, I must admit, I'm not too comfortable with the idea of a conference call to Baxter. The last one was extremely unproductive. What we need is to have some face time with them. See if we can schedule that. And we'll go to them. They need to see our effort. And you're right, adding Johnson is a good call. He's a crackerjack! But I still want a small, tight unit for this meeting. Maybe we can pull McDermott and put him with Sanders to work the Xs and Os of the tax side of this thing. They've worked well together in the past. And I think Baxter will be impressed that we have two units working on their behalf. Yes, let's jump on this.

As you can see by this example, Mr. Davis didn't say yes to everything that Michaels proposed. Nor should he. He didn't like the idea of a conference call and he didn't want to increase the size of the core unit attending the meeting. On these two points he was quite firm. He did, however, say, "Yes . . . And!" to everything else that Michaels proposed.

Simply put, instead of saying no to the entirety of Michaels' plan (as witnessed in example 1) because certain elements didn't work for him, Mr. Davis accepted that there was some inherent relevance to the plan and said "Yes." He then built upon this foundation by saying "and," using it as a springboard to potential solutions. Laid out, in thought sequence, our example would look like this:

- Yes . . . we need to save the Baxter account.
  And . . . we need to meet with them.
  And . . . the last conference call was problematic.
  And . . . therefore, we'll go to them.

- Yes . . . adding Johnson to the team is a good call.
  And . . . I still want a small tight unit for the meeting.
  And . . . McDermott works well with Sanders.
  And . . . Baxter will like that two units are working on their behalf.
  And . . . let's jump on it!

Based on the preceding example, ask yourself once again: "Am I a 'Yes . . . And!' person?" Does your mind operate in this fashion? Do you wait for the whole story, actively listening the entire time and then postulate? Or do you hit the first pothole then quickly sell your car, proclaiming America's streets the worst in the Western world? Speaking of quickly, quickly grab a pen, pencil, or nearby quill and jot down the following phrase: *Yes, I am a "Yes . . . And!" person and here's why.*

Grab your journal and start making a list, check it twice, but by all means, do not be bashful. Remember, this list is for your eyes only. Enter any and all examples of you being a "Yes . . . And!" person and carrying forth that philosophy. Not just today, but as far back as you can remember. Once you've completed your list, or at least made the first pass, go through the entries one at a time and try to recall the situations as they played out.

- Who else was present?
- What was the mood of any other individuals involved?
- How was your "Yes . . . And!" received?
- What did it feel like to be a "Yes . . . And!" person?

If your memory of these events is somewhat cloudy, especially in the areas of the effect your "Yes . . . And!" had on individuals or the group, you're not alone. Sensory awareness is a developed skill. And like anything else, becoming a fully realized "Yes . . . And!" person takes training. Like riding a bike or, wouldn't you know it, improvisation. Over time you develop a feel for it. It becomes as much a sixth sense as anything tangible.

Using your journal, continue to enter the times you make "Yes . . . And!" choices or act in a "Yes . . . And!" manner. Note in detail how you felt and what was happening around you. The more you do it, the keener your perceptions will become. Some of your journal entries may look like this:

Today Bonnie (wife) asked me to pick up the kids after school. (I wanted to say no, but I didn't.) On the way home they wanted to stop at Dairy Queen. (I wanted to go straight home, but I stopped.) I had my first Mister Misty in about ten years. Drank it way too fast and got a brain-ache from the cold. We all had a good laugh. I love to see my children laugh.

If you want to see if this truly fits a "Yes . . . And!" scenario, take your journal entry and rewrite it in the thought sequence fashion we used earlier.

- Yes . . . someone needs to pick up the kids.
  And . . . the Dairy Queen is on the way home.
  And . . . I haven't had a Mister Misty in ages.
  And . . . I forgot that drinking it too fast gives you a brain-ache.
  And . . . my children laughed at my Misty mistake.
  And . . . nothing makes me feel better than seeing my children laugh.

Your journal entry may be much more simple, maybe just a thought or a few words. That's fine, there are no rules about journal entries.

Great, we're starting to scratch the surface of "Yes . . . And!" and its importance when coming face to face with a potential negative business or personal climate. Let's now look at the next small step you can take on your way to becoming a master of the "Yes . . . And!"

Just Say It!

Nike's slogan is very simple, and at the same time very powerful: Just Do It! The message? If you truly want to be the best at anything, you've got to do the work. Our slogan is also very simple and, dare we say, quite powerful, especially in the hands of a fledgling "Yes . . . And!"-er: Just Say It! The message? If you want to be a top "Yes . . . And!" person, you've got to start by saying the words aloud. Don't mumble them, don't whisper them, and don't forget them. The only way to become good at it is to just say them, starting with word one: Yes!

For most people, saying "yes" can be a very difficult proposition. For with that word comes an implied understanding of what is being asked or stated and acknowledgment of commitment. And we all know that commitment can be hard to come by, especially in the corporate world, where saying yes and attaching your name to a project that goes belly-up or a promotion that fizzles can put you under the microscope, making it much less likely that you'll go out on that same limb so readily next time. Instead, you may just quietly slink back into the faceless, nameless background known as middle management—corporate America's version of the witness protection program.

YES! COMPANIES

If you are fortunate, you already work for a company or corporation that makes it easy for its employees to say yes, because the company itself is a yes company. They say yes to forward thinking, they say yes to taking calculated risks, and they say yes to their customers. The more loudly they say it, the more successful they become. And who are some of these yes companies?

- Southwest Airlines
- The Ritz Carlton Hotels
- Pike Place Fish Market (Seattle, Wash.)

Each of these organizations has an air of confidence that comes from knowing that in order to succeed, each and every day they must say yes to the unknown and never look back, never rest on their laurels, and never say never. You want proof? In 1971 Southwest Airlines started with three planes serving three Texas cities. Today, by saying "Yes" to the unexpected, their fleet numbers three hundred aircraft as they continue to expand their horizons and refuse to rest on their laurels. But it's not just about getting bigger . . . it's about getting better. In 1992 Southwest won the first annual airline Triple Crown: best on-time record, best baggage handling, and fewest customer complaints—a feat no other airline has been able to accomplish, not even for a single month. Oh, by the way, they have been profitable for an unprecedented twenty-eight straight years.

In 1965, after watching numerous attempts to sell to out-siders fall short, employee John Yokoyama purchased Pike Place Fish, an unassuming fish market along Seattle's harbor. With just one goal in mind, to become world famous, John set out to redefine Pike Place Fish. Today, his vision has be-come a reality, and the fish aren't just biting—they're flying! The fishmongers actually throw fish to each other, and people crowd around to witness the joyous spectacle. One day, among the crowd were folks from ChartHouse International, the leading producer of corporate learning films. They were so impressed by what they saw that they approached John about doing a video. The result of this inspiration was not just one video but three—*Fish!*, *Fish! Sticks,* and *Fish! Tales* (which are now available in five languages and are the most popular training videos on the planet)—as well as a bestselling book by Stephen C. Lundin, Ph.D., Harry Paul, and John Christensen. In addition to doing incredible business, John and his staff have inspired other organizations to adopt their formula for success: engaging the customer and making every trip to Pike Place Fish a once-in-a-lifetime experience. Not bad for a place that just sells fish. They started by just saying "Yes," and now they can say it in five different languages!

DON'T YOU HATE IT WHEN . . .

The phone rings. You're extremely busy, but you answer anyway. The recorded message says, "Please hold the line for a very important message." Wait, shouldn't the message say, "You are not important enough to receive a call from a human being. Our time is more valuable than yours. Get over it!" Some companies love to say no, others have a machine do it for them.

So, let's put you on that path, the path to being a world-famous "Yes . . . And!" person. The first order of business is to eliminate as many of the prerecorded negative responses in your brain as we can. And since we can't just reach in and pull them out, we must record over them. We must establish a new message.

Yes, Yes, a Thousand Times, Yes. If it's not obvious by now, let's make it crystal clear. We want you to practice saying the word "yes." We want you to say it out loud and continue saying it until it becomes second nature. We want you to say it about yourself, about other people, and about things you hope to complete or accomplish. And being that you're already here, let's start with you.

Mirror, Mirror, on the Wall. Practice doesn't always make perfect, but it does make sense. For the next thirty days, here is your challenge. Every time you pass a mirror in your home we want you to stop, look closely at yourself and say the word "yes." Say it a few times, confidently. Now throw caution to the wind and add a little affirmative nod as you say it. Let your body feel the positive connection between the word and the action. Remember, our actions often speak louder than our words. So, lead with your yes and follow with your nod. Say it and display it. You are slowly and steadily laying the foundation for your brain's new, positive message center.

At some point during this thirty-day period you will start to notice that, outside of your home, any encounter with a mirror, even from a distance, will bring the word "yes" to mind. When this happens, make sure to journal the experience. It is important to note the feelings associated with exercises whenever possible. Remember, improvisation is about constant reinforcement of ideas. Noting experiences is a reinforcement of you.

TIME (GOOFING) OFF FOR GOOD BEHAVIOR

For the good folks at 3M Corporation, creators of Scotch tape and Post-It notes, a little corporate daydreaming is not only accepted, it's expected. Each employee is informed upon hiring that 15 percent of their work day (that's about an hour and a half of an eight-hour day) is free time to be spent at their discretion, using their creative imagination. No, it's not time for employees to roll out a nap mat, but it is unstructured, with no one is looking over your shoulder, cracking the "let's get creative" whip. 3M realizes that this not only helps individuals truly touch base with their unique creativity, it also helps the company retain its employees and better serve its customers. 3M can't say who will dream up the next zillion-dollar idea, but they can and do say, "Yes . . . And!" to anyone who wants to try.

TIPS ON THE TOPIC

- Replace "No!," "Yes, but . . . ," and "Yes, or . . ." with "Yes . . . And!" to keep the doors of exploration and possibilities wide open.
- "Yes!" is more definitive than other seemingly positive responses: "okay," "sure," "all right," etc. Use "Yes!"
- Practice, practice, practice.
- Eliminate the "Been there, done that" mentality, which diminishes potential.

PERSONAL EXERCISE 6
Bedtime Story

The Players: You and your child, or niece or nephew.

The Object: To improvise a five-minute bedtime story. One of the simplest, but sometimes most intimidating parts of improvising is storytelling. As "mature" working adults we are generally more comfortable spouting facts about an Internet stock offering than waxing poetic about a bunny dancing through a purple forest. Well, give it a shot. Improvising a story for a child takes away the fear of your "first draft" being judged. (What's the worst that can happen? Your son is eleven and he wants to hear a story about an Internet stock offering, or—he falls asleep.)

How to: 1. Tuck the little darling in, turn off the lights, and close your eyes. Ask the child to pick the "hero" or "heroine" of the story and in what warm, fuzzy, spooky, or funny location the story takes place. Say "Yes" to each suggestion, even if your son suggests "a ninja kung fu Uzi-wielding street fighter in a virtual-reality cyber hell." Then say ". . . And!" and add to his suggestion. Go with it.

2. Just tell the story.

3. Tips: Be as descriptively detailed as possible. Use dialogue. Improvise character voices. You know you have them in you!

A Twist: As you make up a bedtime story, stop in mid-sentence and ask your child to fill in the "blank." For instance, "The story of Archibald the Raccoon and the magical trash can takes place in a forest. The trees in this forest aren't brown and green, they are _____." Whatever he or she says, accept it as the best idea in the world ("Yes") and incorporate it into the tall tale (. . . And!).

The Result: A children's book deal worth $1.8 million, not including the Happy Meal action figure rights. Or, a heightened ability to trust your imagination and spontaneity, which is the bedrock of "Yes . . . And!" and thinking on your feet.

IMPROVISE THIS!

AN INSIDE TIP FROM OUTSIDE THE BOX

MELISSA PETERMAN

Actress

Melissa Peterman is a stage, film, and television comedy actress on the rise. Her background in improvisation includes over six hundred performances in the hit play *Tony n' Tina's Wedding*. She is also a veteran company member at the renowned Brave New Workshop in Minneapolis, where she performed and wrote improv-based comedy and satire, along with teaching the craft of improvisation acting. Now based in L.A., her credits include the academy award–winning film *Fargo* and the Oxygen channel sketch comedy show *Running with Scissors*. Melissa is currently a costar on *Reba* on WB.

Q: Melissa. You seem to us to be a natural improvisational performer. Were you "that kind of kid"?

A: *Well, I was a bizarre child . . . I had a big imagination. I was perfectly fine playing by myself and had a huge cast of characters always around me that I talked to. I didn't mind being alone, because I wasn't alone. In fact for about a year, I had a paper frog that I talked to . . . I didn't need a lot of toys. I knew as a young kid that I wanted to perform.*

Q: Did you take any improv classes?

A: *Yes. In college I took improv workshops. And the* Tony n' Tina's Wedding *rehearsal process was learning improv structures.*

Q: So, what happened after you declared yourself, and became a professional actor?

A: *The first thing I booked after college was the movie* Fargo. *Then I booked* Tony n' Tina's Wedding *in Minneapolis. It was almost all improv. We had an outline from the New York production, and that outline didn't always translate to the Midwest. We had so much freedom. The character that I played had no written lines.*

Q: And what character was that?

A: *I was always this character, Maddy—stripper / Mary Kay consultant / pleasure advocate. On any given night, since it was all improvised, whatever happened to me personally that day might affect what my character did that night onstage. I knew this character so well I could do anything. One day I fell down the stairs at home and had bruises, so that night my character talked to the audience about how she got them kickboxing . . .*

Q: Here's a segue—does your improvisation experience affect you offstage?

A: *If I weren't an actor, that skill [improvisation] would be valuable anyway. I'm better at job interviews, I'm better at coming into a roomful of strangers, I'm better at parties, I'm better at meeting people, just because I have the confidence that whatever happens, I'm going to be okay. I don't feel I can get thrown very easily in a lot of situations.*

Q: How does the *"fear of improvising"* factor come into play for you?

A: *A part of it is very scary. Fear of taking that jump—that you might fail and fall flat on your face because the situation may go south. To trust yourself that whatever comes out of your mouth, whether it's really brilliant or stupid, it's still going to be okay.*

Q: Has going with "whatever comes out of your mouth," that first impulse, ever gone south for you?

A: *Oh that's never happened to me. I usually nail things immediately, first time. "One take Peterman"—that's me! (Laughing) No, that happens a lot. I think you have to go into improvising knowing that it's going to go south a lot of times, but you just have to believe it's going to be fine. It's going to be okay. People respect you when you say what your impulse is, what you really mean.*

Q: Do you think there's one key improvisation ideal, one concept, that you'd like to share? This may be a loaded question.

A: *I know it's a cliché, but it's saying "Yes."*

Q: Good. Because that's a chapter in our book.

A: *Is it? Oh there was no coaxing there. (Laughs again) My biggest pet peeve is somebody who says "No" and negates. It stops the scene, it stops the learning process. It stops everything. If you just say "Yes," no matter how ridiculous it seems, the situation is going to go further and you're going to learn something. Train yourself to say "Yes." I think that's so huge. As an actress, in any audition situation, if I didn't have that training to say yes, I would never get hired. Ever. When you walk in and have your set idea of what that character's like, and they want something completely different—If I said no or my body said "I can't," I wouldn't get hired.*

"Yes . . . And!"

Q: "Active listening." Important?

A: *I'm sorry. What did you say? (Laughing) Ahh, I should save it for the show. It's right up there with saying "Yes." In life and onstage— when people aren't listening, there's no real moving forward, no communication. Again, everything stops. I try to test people to see if they're looking me in the eye, or over my shoulder. I say, "Excuse me, I'm on fire. Could you bring some water over here?" To see if they react, if they're really listening.*

Q: As both a performer and a person with a real life, how would you define improvisation?

A: *Improv is not all about "funny." It's about being aware, and open and listening and saying yes to things . . . The idea of improv is just to be an aware and listening person who is willing to go and play and go places. Or, I'm going to go wherever you lead me, and I'm going to follow my impulse, and say "Yes."*

Q: What about living "in the moment"?

A: *It's a hard thing for an improviser. There's my inner voice, I'll call her Miranda, that starts to plan the scene or the situation. Ninety-nine percent of the time, those scenes will fail. I'm not looking and listening and just reacting to what I'm given. I'm planning what's going to happen. Or [in everyday life] I'm going to plan how this date is going to go or this meeting . . . you realize you can't. You're not a puppeteer for everyone's life. I'm not saying you shouldn't be prepared. But when something unplanned happens in that meeting for instance, you have the tools to say, "Okay. All right. I didn't expect that to happen. I can change. I'll be flexible." That's very important.*

Q: Last question, Melissa. What would you say to someone just about to experience improvisation?

A: *First off, you already have it in you. Go for it. Anybody and everybody can do it. Don't listen to my voice Miranda. You have nothing to lose, and it's a skill that will carry you through anything. Whether it's just to be better at life or in a job interview, to feel more confident walking into a room, or actually onstage performing on* Whose Line Is It Anyway? *It's fun and easy. Improv is a skill you need to practice all the time. It's like any other muscle. If you don't exercise it, it goes away.*

SEVEN

PRO CHOICES: THE RIGHT TO LAUGH

Stop. Don't do another thing until you do this exercise. Think about the last time you laughed hysterically. You gasped for air and almost (maybe you did, but want to keep it to yourself) wet your pants. The kind of laugh where you threw your head back and laughed so hard not a sound came out. Then, you stopped laughing, and only minutes later burst into hysterics again, only to be followed by a foot-pounding tribal dance. Who were you with? What were you doing? How did it make you feel?

If the only memory you can recollect is of being in church miming obscene gestures with Barbie and Ken on the front pew while the priest was giving his sermon, it might be a good time to pause and reflect. (Which is quite different from pausing and genuflecting, like you were supposed to be doing.) Laughter, playfulness, and fun in your life will not only help you to enjoy your life more, it will make others enjoy being around you more.

Finding humor in your life and being humorous have tremendous value. Laughter is to our mental health what physical exercise is to our body. Same benefits, minus the Stairmaster. Freud said, "Wit can express inhibited tendencies like the desire to act our regressive infantile sexual or aggressive behavior. A lack of humor can be a sign of mental illness." So if you don't want people to stop by your cubicle and hear you sing: "They're coming to take me away ha ha ho ho hee hee, to the funny farm where life is beautiful all the time . . ." we suggest you spend some time flexing your humor muscles.

Sources of laughter are endless. You may get a really good laugh every time you take a look at your business plan. Or when you take out your high school pictures and you notice your hair didn't fit in the school photo. If you can't remember the last time you burst into hysterics, break out the Pledge and dust off your sense of humor.

Being deadly serious can make you the Jack Kevorkian of any creative environment. In this chapter we'll explore how:

- Improvisers learn to loosen up, get out of their heads, and get loopy.
- To lighten up and explore how laughter and play can improve your creativity, health, and wealth.

If you need something to do to get you in the mood to laugh right away, simply take off your clothes and stand in front of the mirror buck-naked. If you're anything like us, that simple vision should provide gales of laughter.

Kids Have All the Fun

Studies show that children laugh about four hundred times a day. As adults we squeak out maybe fifteen chuckles. That means that kids laugh about thirty times more than we do! Why is that? It has a lot to do with the amount of time we play in a day. The amount of time we engage in activities that allow us freedom to laugh and goof off. And what sort of people we surround ourselves with.

In our playshops we allow people to break out of their everyday routines and help them to turn their focus on play. In a playful environment people can stretch their creative muscles and have fun, all the while creating a sense of community. If you don't think it's possible for grown-ups to play with their colleagues at work, picture this:

CHOMP

Four hundred top executives from an insurance agency are gathered together to focus on customer service and sales. Jim, our consummate "conductor," asks the audience if they've seen the Broadway musical *Stomp*. He then goes on to explain that because we're in a banquet room just about to eat lunch, we will do a variation on *Stomp* called *Chomp*. He asks everyone to take something from their table to make noise with—forks, spoons, glasses, etc. Our keyboardist starts playing a percussive beat. Each table is a unit and, as such, is asked to make their own music. As Jim conducts the silverware orchestra, people's faces begin to lighten up, there is an electric energy in the room; everyone is fully involved and contributes. Jim goes to tables one by one, and holds the microphone out as the selected group plays. A hush falls over the rest of the room and, one at a time, each table takes the spotlight.

Jim returns to the stage and the entire four hundred—person silverware orchestra plays. The "music" is electrifying. There is not one person in the room who isn't involved. Jim has the group play softer (think of the song "Shout"—A little bit softer now . . .), and the room becomes powerfully silent. Then, as if on cue, the audience claps and whistles and gives themselves a standing ovation.

If you were now thinking to yourself, "Has the world gone mad? Why would a company pay good money for that?" Well yes, the world has gone mad, but we'd like to focus on why a company would do this. Here's why. When a group of people has a shared experience of fun and creative play, change occurs. People start to see things differently. After we have a group do an activity like this, we hear comments such as, "That was great," and "I haven't had that much fun in a long time." And we know, as do these companies, that people who enjoy one another and who can have fun together make better teams and get more done, which results in a better bottom line.

Commonality

When people participate in play together they create something called "commonality." Commonality is a shared experience that everyone can relate to. A good example of commonality is the personal joke. You know the jokes, the ones where you and another person, or group of people, say something that conjures up a collective memory and you all laugh. All of you laugh—except the sorry new person who wasn't there to experience what you did. He sits on the outside, just not "getting it." Commonalities can take relationships to the next level and they are often used as story lines for our favorite shows.

"A Little Song, a Little Dance, a Little Seltzer Down Your Pants."

If you don't remember this line (or are too young to have seen it), it's from one of the all-time classic episodes of the *Mary Tyler Moore Show,* "Chuckles Bites the Dust." This episode starts with the tragic revelation that beloved Chuckles the Clown was crushed to death by an elephant while dressed as a peanut. (An all too common death among clowns.) Go ahead, laugh, it's okay. Laughing at inappropriate times is human nature. Which is why we can understand Mary's coworkers Ted, Murray, Sue Ann, and Lou's reaction to the news at the office—muffled giggles, snorts, repressed guffaws, pursed lips, and finally, outbursts of unbridled laughter. All under the scornful and judgmental eye of Mary Richards. We watch and we laugh. The reason we laugh so hard at this episode is we've all been there. We have all experienced a time when it was just not appropriate to laugh—but we did anyway, and we couldn't stop ourselves. Now, had Mary involved herself in the laughter that went on back at the office when everyone first learned of Chuckles's death, the unthinkable wouldn't have happened. But it did. In the middle of the tenderest moment of Chuckles's funeral, Mary went on an uncontrollable laughing jag that she couldn't stop. Until of course the minister told her that it was what Chuckles would have wanted, at which time Mary burst into tears.

Laughing at inappropriate times is uniquely human and highlights our imperfection. And it falls directly into the category of "commonality."

DID YOU KNOW?

Recently an article in *Alternative Therapies in Health and Medicine* research concluded with this quotation: "A merry heart doeth good like a medicine but a broken spirit drieth the bone."—Proverbs 17:22. Or, it is good for us to laugh whether an elephant crushes a clown . . . or just his peanuts.

When we're released from our corporate roles and images and we are allowed to play, we laugh. Laughter is the natural byproduct of play. When we play during improvisation we never know what will happen, and people laugh at the unexpected, the surprise.

Creating commonalities is good business. Laughing at inappropriate times is not. It's just something we do. Companies know that commonality is good and that's why there are company picnics, bowling leagues, internal company newsletters, and humor bulletin boards. And it's why everyone laughs when they remember the CEO tripping as she walked onstage to address the company at the annual meeting. (And why they still giggle every time they see her in "those shoes.") Through shared experiences we create memories. People in every level of business know that having fun once in a while is good for relieving stress.

Stressing Fun

In any beginning improvisation class filled with both actors and laypeople, you will find varying levels of uptight individuals—some people who are guarded, stiff, and afraid to laugh and others who are happy, fun-loving, and willing to share their Prozac. By the end of the fifth or sixth week of classes there is a profound change in this newly found circle of friends. There is synergy, trust, and an enormous amount of laughter—from everyone. When people have fun together as a group by doing exercises and playing games, they loosen up and the result is a productive, creative team.

YOU KNOW THE DRILL

My Name is . . .
You're going to need a partner for this.

You and your partner face each other. You both start the game by saying (in unison and in rhythm, punctuated by snapping fingers): "My name is, (snap) my name is (snap)." Three times. One of you—let's say you—now make up a name (first and last): Tom Gigglesnort.

Now your partner must complete the first round by telling us what this person's occupation is—it needn't make sense, but it must use the initials of the made-up person's name. In this case, T. G. So your partner might say: "and I Tidy up Gutters!"

Or: "and I Titillate Grapefruit."

Then begin again with both players saying, in unison and with snaps, "My name is, my name is," with your partner now making up a name and you supplying the occupation.

Keep going as long as you can, alternating each time and picking up the pace as you continue.

"My name is, my name is, my name is Smuggly Brightwhite. And I . . ." Quick, improvise three occupations using the initials *S* and *B!*

Laugh It Up

It is said that laughter is the shortest distance between two people. This is proven in improvisation classes, in corporate America, and between flirting couples in bars across the nation on a daily basis. But many of us simply don't take time to laugh and enjoy our world, or we've forgotten how. Too many people fill their moments with deadlines instead of laugh lines. We believe that we can control the amount of laughter and play in our lives. (If you're reading this in a foxhole in Kosovo, we understand we're going to be receiving some letters.) Enjoying life, laughing, and becoming a playful person may take some practice. It may take the ability to look at yourself closely and examine which elements of your life are fun and enjoyable and which are *booooring* and deadly serious. To truly enjoy life takes the ability to take your job seriously but take yourself lightly. Hmmm, where have you heard that before?

> Most of the time I don't have much fun.
> The rest of the time I don't have any fun at all.
> —Woody Allen

Leader of the Pack

If you are the leader of an organization, then you are already in a position to create change in your environment, to take a "fun workplace" inventory and begin making changes where they need to be made and build on people's strengths—starting with yourself.

Recently we did a "performance keynote" and playshop for three hundred leaders of a major HMO in California. As the curtain went up at the conference at a Disneyland hotel, music started and the CEO of the HMO (we know, enough with the acronyms) came out with huge white Mickey Mouse hands on and danced onstage in front of his staff.

He was clearly taking a risk *and* having a good time in the process. The leaders in the audience loved it. They loved him for being playful and fun and mostly for giving them permission to follow suit. This is no stupid CEO. Endorphins were flying about like pixie dust, as well as creative ideas. And camaraderie was building in this HMO faster than you can make a copayment. How did this CEO decide to wear huge white gloves and dance around? In a meeting where improvisation mixed with heavy dose of "Yes . . . And!" produced "Hey, why don't we . . ." Having fun, creating something together, and taking risks is powerful and memorable.

Creative leaders can make the ordinary extraordinary. And some have made humor and laughter a deliberate corporate strategy. Through the spontaneity of serious playfulness, people tap into personal solutions and can envision pathways that weren't evident when they were holed up in their cubicle, one yellowed Dilbert cartoon as inspiration.

There are companies that are downright brain dead when it comes to laughter and play in their work environment. And you know what the difference is between the mindset of a business that encourages laughter and play and one that encourages watching the clock and serious business: Profits. Employee turnover costs beaucoup bucks and a loyal customer is priceless.

The word is out that people like to work in a playful environment. Let's listen in on a recent interview at Andy's Gas and Goods:

MANAGER: Welcome to Andy's Gas and Goods. Why are you interested in working here, Stu?

APPLICANT: I heard that you are one of the 4 percent of companies that have a humor consultant on staff. And, that you're one of the 8 percent that include humor in your mission statement and values. That's important to me.

MANAGER: Yes, that's true, Stu. Hey that rhymes—let's get that in the company newsletter! Anyway Stu, we feel that if you're happy and have a balanced life you'll be more productive, which in turn helps our bottom line. So Stu, you don't mind working hard if you enjoy your work?

APPLICANT: No, just like most people I want to be appreciated and have fun with my fellow coworkers.

MANAGER: That's great, Stu. With that kind of an attitude I'm going to offer you double the salary we usually pay for this job!

APPLICANT: There's a salary?

Okay, Stu may be overly anxious to be in a fun environment. And he may lack the drive to earn a good living. But Stu, like other people, just wants to have some fun every day. And companies like Andy's Gas and Goods know if they provide that kind of atmosphere they'll attract people with a sense of humor and a lighthearted attitude, which will translate into less turnover and better customer service. Companies like Southwest Airlines, Caribou Coffee, and Kaiser Permanente Health Plan–Hospitals, California, all look for a sense of humor in their applicants. And by showing a little personality you stand out from the crowd and can create a positive feeling within the company. So, what can you do to show your sense of humor and create a playful environment? What can you do at work to live the spirit of improvisation, laughter, and fun? And how can you accomplish this without using plastic dog vomit or leaving a fish to rot under the seat of your boss's Mercedes?

Work to the Top of Your Intelligence

One way to raise the level of your ability to find unique humor in the world around you is to follow the path of the most successful improvisers and work to the top of your intelligence. Working to the top of your intelligence doesn't necessarily mean making oblique references about the political chaos in Costa Rica or going on a diatribe about how DNA molecules break down during stress. It simply requires you to pass on the obvious, easy marks (blond jokes and potty humor) and seek out the irony or satirical potential of a situation or scenario. It makes the work a little harder, but the payoff is much more satisfying and rewarding. Here are just a couple of routines that we ask improvisers to consider as part of their performance preparation.

- Read the daily newspaper—not just the sports section or the comic strips. Share what you've read with other performers before a show. (Commonality)
- Buy a book of crossword puzzles and work on them occasionally. An increased vocabulary can lead to having the perfect word at the right time—not just one that suffices.
- Read the works of distinctly different authors and playwrights. This helps improv actors feel comfortable in many different styles of performance, allowing them to work at a higher level of proficiency and to the top of their intelligence.

Follow the best improvisers and take the high road, leaving the whoopee cushion in the hands of others—not on the chair where your secretary sits.

- Institute a "Children's Hour." Have someone do a Dairy Queen run, then shut off the phones, eat, laugh, and get loopy. Do impressions of customers, coworkers, and vendors. (The late Minnesota Vikings Pro Bowl offensive lineman Korey Stringer was known and loved in the locker room for doing wicked impressions of players that immediately lightened the mood of any tense situation.)
- Remove the magazines from the coworker and customer lounge. Create a basket full of toys: Legos, Mr. Potato Head, Magic 8 Ball, Rubik's Cube, and Etch-a-Sketch. (Bonus: if you happen to have a nanny cam, this could provide hours of fun for the company party.)
- Champagne Fridays (not to be confused with casual Fridays). Celebrate your week by toasting one another and discussing the week's highlights. Nonalcohol option: 7-Up served in fluted champagne glasses. (Presentation is everything.)
- Put up a bulletin board with the company's holiday photos. Add captions to them.
- Wear a tool belt around the office. Don't say anything about it.
- Create a new internal message or question of the day, one that your coworkers will get a kick out of and that will add an element of play to their day. A great starting point would be comedian Steven Wright's material: "Why do they have Braille keypads on ATM drive-up windows?" Discussion will be held in room 210 at 11:12.
- Change a colleague's (friend's) screen saver to an outrageous *National Enquirer* headline featuring a photo of him or her.
- Ask for a raise by writing a funny poem about it. "'Twas the

night before my performance review and all through the office, not a raise was stirring, not even a bonus."

• Offer to be the trainer (remember breaking barriers? You can do this) at the next new coworker orientation. Design a fun program including a scavenger hunt, crossword puzzle, and improv game.

The Home Version

• The next time she makes you angry, send your sister a cookie bouquet that says: "Bite Me."
• Open up a "complaint desk." Complaints from children, partner, or spouse will be listened to and considered between the hours of 8:00–8:30 A.M. Monday and Friday. Advanced version: All complaints must be submitted in the form of a limerick.
• To warn family members if you're in a bad mood, drink out of evil character mugs featuring such characters as the Queen from *Snow White,* the Riddler from *Batman,* Cruella De Vil from *101 Dalmatians.*

You can have fun with virtually any situation (within reason) if you look at it from another perspective. Stand outside of the problem or opportunity and try to figure out ways you can break out of the same ol', same ol' and have some fun. And, in order to play well with others, you must get out of your head. Give yourself permission to take a break from your responsibilities and the pressures of everyday life.

Tune In

Play and laughter at work and at home can be achieved by paying attention to your environment, to your moods, and to those around you. By being in the moment you will start to see and feel the energy in the room, the aura of the people around you, and discover its source. You will start to see how you contribute to the "mood," if you will. (Remember "Theme Song" from chapter 4?) You can control the amount of mirth in your environment by becoming aware of your own mood and the control you have over changing it.

So, now that you know the positive effects of laughing on health and wealth, you're going to have to control your inner thoughts from saying, "Well, I was funny and fun to be with on Thursday and no one else was, so that's the last time I'm going to be fun." Now you're just being a jerk and that's icky—so *stop it*. Start being more of the person who commits to mirth and is the leader (think of yourself as the Control Central of Happiness) and eventually it will catch on. In the worst possible scenario, let's say no one else catches your fire . . . you at least will be at a better place. And that's good.

> Life is too short and too hard and too serious
> not to be humorous about it.
> —Herb Kelleher, founder, Southwest Airlines

Laughter and having a lighthearted outlook on things can also work in tough customer situations. Here's an example we love. In corporate speak this goes under, "How to reframe a negative situation." On a busy day boarding passengers onto a flight at a large airline, a check-in clerk had her wits about her and was in true form. A gentleman, actually nix the gentle part, didn't like the amount of time it was taking to find out if he was going to get a seat in first-class. He was slowly growing more and more irritable and decided to take it out on the clerk. So he walked up to her station, slammed his fist on the podium, and said, "Do you know who I am? Do you have any idea who I am?" And she (you're gonna love this) picked up her microphone and said, "Does anyone know who this man is? He doesn't seem to know who he is." You can imagine the positive reaction this got from the remaining passengers, who were also waiting. Now there's a woman who was thinking on her feet!

Here's the great thing. She didn't get fired (so the story goes), and she probably didn't go home with an ulcer either. She helped the other passengers go home without an ulcer and gave them a great story to tell around the dinner table. People with a sense of humor, who can laugh at themselves and with others, are just plain fun to be around. And they're great at easing tension.

Get a Humor Buddy

In order to be spontaneous and play with your friends, your colleagues, and your customers, you'll have to be able to physically relax. Wait! Before you run off to your massage therapist for a quick aromatherapy session or reach for a martini (although occasionally both are swell ideas), try this: Put yourself in a playful mood by putting on some fun music and dancing or walking in s-l-o-w m-o-t-i-o-n or calling someone who you know will make you laugh. In fact, we recommend having a "humor buddy"! Someone who you can count on to make you laugh and put you in a humorous frame of mind. If you don't have one—get one. Pay attention to who makes you laugh, who you have fun with, and try to involve them in your life. And sometimes, if we're lucky, our humor buddies are right under our noses. We might be wearing the ring they gave us a very, very long time ago. They're probably just hidden under mortgage payments, soccer games, and clogged toilets. With a good cleaning and a little attention, they're good as new.

The more you engage in activities that relax you and help you to be more playful, the more opportunities you will see in your home and work environment to laugh and play. When you are aware of the opportunities it's easier to act on them. Many improv actors loosen up before their shows with some playful activity. Students of improvisation begin their classes by loosening up through gibberish games, movement exercises, or one we love called "Zip Zap Zop," which you'll find in the Epilogue.

YOU ONLY LIVE ONCE—LIGHTEN UP!

Molly: Here's an example of a spontaneous combustion moment—a moment of unplanned playfulness: My daughter, Christina, and I were washing my car one summer afternoon in a self-serve car wash, where you insert a dollar bill and get a thimble of water. I had a lot on my mind: busy, busy, busy, work, work, work. Christina had a lot on her mind: fun, fun, fun, play, play, play. (She was eight years old.) It was irritating me that she wasn't paying attention to what she was doing and wasn't cleaning the car the way I wanted. Apparently quite fed up with my "sunny disposition," she looked at me à la Jack Nicholson from *The Shining* and with total commitment and passion, nailed me from head to toe with the hose. I was shocked and soaked. I couldn't talk. She was laughing so hard I considered calling 911—then we both went into hysterics. Then the man behind us, who was clearly in the work, work, work mode, told us to "Knock it off!" Christina then sprayed the water on herself, pointed it at me again, and well, from that point on we just couldn't stop laughing. And here's the fun part: The work, work, work man started laughing too! And you know, to this day (eight years later), it is still one of our favorite memories.

Fun doesn't have to be scheduled. Playing together is one of the quickest ways to make a connection. And we can make it happen almost any time, anywhere. Playfulness keeps couples together, families close, and companies creative. But if our lips are pursed and our cheeks (the ones below the waist) can securely hold a dime, we're not going to be open to the possibilities and opportunities that present themselves. Smile, relax, and heck, you just might drop some change.

> It's amazing how long it takes to change something
> you're not working on.
> —R. D. Clyde

Remember what Emily Dickinson said? Of course you don't, unless you are currently in the ninth grade. We'll refresh your memory: "That it will never come again is what makes life so sweet." The opportunity to have fun and be more playful presents itself every day in one form or another. No opportunity will ever present itself the same way again. So it is up to you to seize the moment. Seize the day. *Carpe Diem*. It is up to you to find opportunities to laugh and play . . . and to connect with others.

It's up to you to figure out how serious you want to be. If you could lighten up just a bit, you would reap the benefits of that choice. As Mel Brooks said, "Now thyself" is more important than "Know thyself." Get going!

TIPS ON THE TOPIC

- Laughter is to our mental health what physical exercise is to our body. Seek out a humor buddy.
- Engage in fun, playful activities as often as you can.
- Play improv games such as, "My name is . . ." to help you think on your feet.
- Bring the spirit of improvisation and fun to your work. Stop what you are doing and dazzle your coworkers with an impression or a spontaneous game.

PERSONAL EXERCISE 7
Fun with Telemarketers!

The Players: You and an unsuspecting telemarketer who calls you, as usual, just as you're sitting down to dinner.

The Object: To spontaneously create a new personality for yourself while interacting with a telemarketer.

With all due respect to the telemarketing industry—we all hate telemarketers. Every last one of them. Why not use this golden and far-too-frequent opportunity to work on your improvisation skills?

How To: 1. When a telemarketer calls—and let's just say she's from a phone company—choose an emotion to color all your answers to her questions. Happy, skeptical, completely dumbfounded, angry, or confused. No premeditation allowed— just act! If an Irish or German accent comes to you as an inspiration, use it. (Come on— remember. You'll never speak to this person again in your life.)

2. Ask any question at all that pops into your head. For example, "If I decide to sign up with your long distance company, will you give me twelve free oil changes and tire rotations like Sprint did?" Or, "You know I've been with your company before, and I got terrible headaches when I talked on the phone long distance. Have you cleared up that problem?"

The Result: Vengeance.

And this is absolutely free training for you *and* the telemarketer: They'll learn to deal with all sorts of customers, and you'll have a fabulous fun-filled on-the-spot improvisation class.

FOOLPROOF WAYS TO IMPROVISE YOUR WAY OUT OF ANY SITUATION

Take a brief respite from your improvisation education to peruse these scenarios, which range from the ridiculous to the "Hey, I've had that happen." We'll share our somewhat warped responses to a variety of situations that could make a grown man cry . . . if he was a sissy. From being caught locked out of your hotel room in just a towel to mocking your mother-in-law, who happens to be standing right behind you, **Foolproof Ways to Improvise** will give you some insight into how empowering a pithy reply or stuffing a goldfish up your nose can be. *Note:* Although using a Pepperidge Farm Goldfish is much less dramatic, it still can be effective.

It is important to remember that any attempt to improvise your way out from under the microscope must be done with a brazen sense of false bravado, the stamina to hang in there (it could get deep), and if all else fails, the ability to wet yourself on command. And just where is a good place to wet yourself? Depends.

Example 1

Your boss returns early from his vacation and drops by the office to see how things are going. He finds you sitting on the Xerox machine making photocopies of your posterior. His eyes lock on you as he screams, "What in the hell is going on here?" So, what do you do? Well, here are a couple of improvisation options:

- Tell him the company just switched over to an HMO and from now on all employees must do their own X-rays.

- Lie down, pull the copier cover over you, and in a chipmunk voice say, "Look, I'm a sandwich!"
- Jump down, turn your back to him, bend over, and in a commanding voice simply say, "Butt out."

Example 2

You call in sick on Friday so you can finally finish your new family room, but later that day you unexpectedly run into four coworkers at a Sears store. You, in shorts and a T-shirt, are carrying two gallons of paint, four brushes, and a large tarp. They, in suits and power ties, are there for a business meeting you were also supposed to attend. But you forgot. What now?

- Laugh hard, then sheepishly remark, "I thought this meeting was supposed to be casual dress."
- Hand out the paint brushes and exclaim, "Look, everybody uses PowerPoint, let's be different!"
- Stand on the paint cans, wrap the tarp around you, hold a brush up high in the air, and in a husky woman's voice emote, "Bring us your poor, your tired huddled masses . . ."

Example 3

You take one bite of your mother-in-law's infamous "tuna surprise" and promptly spit it right back out. Much to your and the tuna's surprise, it overshoots your plate and lands directly on your mother-in-law's pristine pink pump. Trouble in the henpecked house? We'd say so, unless of course you're quick enough to . . .

- Hit the deck and scream, "It's coming from the grassy knoll!"
- Turn to the closest person and calmly reply, "In Kuala Lumpur, country of my heritage, it is the greatest compliment one can give another. The lower it hits on the leg, the higher the compliment!"
- Pretend to almost faint, let your eyes roll up in your head, and report, in an affected Southern lilt, "Oh my God, it's Flipper . . . I taste Flipper!"

Now, it's your turn. Read the following scenario and then come up with three choice improvisation responses. Take your time. Explore the possibilities. Mix and match. The secret is getting your mind to think in a nontraditional fashion.

Example 4

Your spouse, significant other, or best friend steps out of the changing room wearing a huge grin and something so offensive to all that is tasteful that you cannot help but laugh out loud. The object of your laughter recoils and demands to know the intention of your outburst. You're trying to think on your feet, but one of them is stuffed firmly in your mouth. It's the moment of truth, or in this case . . . lie, deflection, or survival of the fittest.

So, what fits here?

- _____
- _____
- _____

AN INSIDE TIP FROM OUTSIDE THE BOX

Lorna Landvik

Novelist and Improviser

Lorna Landvik has been nominated three times for a Minnesota Book Award ("always a bridesmaid, never a bride") and has won several Loft/McKnight Awards, including an Award of Distinction. Novels of hers that grace the bookshelves are *Patty Jane's House of Curl, Your Oasis on Flame Lake, The Tall Pine Polka,* and *Welcome to the Great Mysterious.* A mother of two, and significant other to one, Lorna also creates and performs her own one-woman plays, some of which are completely improvised.

Q: Lorna, could you describe for us what your journey to becoming a writer was like?

A: *Sure. Having wanted to be a writer since I learned how to read, it nevertheless took me a while to "settle down" to write my first novel. Up to that point I wrote a lot of short fiction and performance pieces, but in my twenties I was too distracted by Hollywood and the Big Movie Career I thought I wanted (Meryl Streep's in particular). It took going on a nine-month peace march (L.A. to Washington, D.C.) to make me realize I really wanted to write novels. (Nine-month peace marches tend to clarify a lot of things.) I have been writing ever since.*

Q: Before you became a novelist you were a stand-up comedian in L.A., and then moved into improvised comedy and satire. Now you write and perform one-woman shows, some of them improvised. What drew you to improv?

A: *I hated doing the same thing (onstage) week after week—and I never did. I'd write a new routine and every week they'd tell me, "You've got to work on your material and hone it." I didn't like doing that. I like the risk involved in improv—playing with other people. What are they going to do? What am I going to do? What did we do together?*

Q: What do you enjoy about performing your improv-based one-woman shows? It seems like you take a huge risk on stage every performance.

A: *I love not knowing what's going to happen next. I love creating a character and situation from audience suggestions and the tightrope one walks—Aghhh, am I gonna fall? If I do fall, will I be able to bounce back? It's my way of skydiving without having to jump out of an airplane.*

Q: And has all of this improv experience affected your life as a novelist?

A: *I think I'm less afraid to try different approaches. My second book is narrated in five different voices, including two men's. I also realize if something isn't working, I can change it.*

Q: Lorna, does practicing and playing with improvisation professionally affect your personal life?

A: *I have a great appreciation for fun. I have on occasion assumed a different identity while chatting with someone in a checkout line, etcetera—just to jazz things up a bit. I've also been known to embarrass my kids with this sort of behavior, but what the hey—*

kids are embarrassed by their parents no matter what we do, so we may as well have fun doing it!

Q: What do you think are the most important things that the average person can gain from taking a risk and jumping into the icy waters of improv?

A: *I think there would be a sense of play and a sense of possibility—"What would happen if I did things this way?" Improv teaches you to expect the unexpected.*

Q: In your opinion is there a certain type of person who embraces an "improvisational" lifestyle?

A: *Probably someone who wants to have fun and appreciates life's wild wooliness.*

Q: Finally—and we always ask this, Lorna—can anyone benefit from learning to improvise?

A: *Yes. I taught an improv workshop for Target stores employees, for example—and they loved it. Everyone is drawn to the arts, if you scratch deep enough to their core and get rid of their fears. And I used to teach improv at my daughter's school. I was always surprised when a kid who was so withdrawn would flower onstage. I think people just want the opportunity and the excuse to play and have fun!*

EIGHT

PARTLY CLOUDY WITH A CHANCE OF BRAINSTORMS

Creative Meeting of the Minds

I am not young enough to know everything.

—Oscar Wilde

A child rips the beautiful wrapping paper from the box as quickly and cleanly as a buzzard with its prey. Inside this box awaits the toy that will make this child the envy of the cul-de-sac. With the blinding speed of L. Jack Horner, the little girl's arm reaches in and pulls out the plum: a porcelain doll that is not only seemingly authentic, but has the fake birth certificate to prove it. The little towheaded girl screams with delight.

Twenty minutes later the doll is still the same beautiful doll she has always been. But the box it came in, oh that box has changed. The box has been a boat, a picnic table, a bed, a trampoline, and even a casket from *Buffy the Vampire Slayer*. Slumped in the corner the discarded doll's eyes seem to say, "Well, just drive a stake through my heart and watch me turn to dust. Don't worry, you can use the your box bulldozer to scoop me up!" How quickly pretty becomes petty.

Children possess an uncanny ability to be creative. Unfortunately, by the time they reach adulthood, job searches, divorces, jail time, and reality television have systematically emptied them of creativity and replaced it with practicality. Most adults have forgotten the wondrous joys of the fertile imagination. They've lost their daring and accepted their self-imposed limitations. So, how do you see the world? What are your perceptions?

A TRUE STORY

The speaker stood before the group of approximately one hundred people and asked, "Who here knows how to sing?" About ten hands slowly went up. "Who here knows how to dance?" he queried. This time about seven or eight hands went up. "How many of you are painters?" he mused. Two hands went up, shyly. The next day this same speaker spoke to a different group, also numbering about one hundred people. The questions were the same. "Who here knows how to sing?" In an instant every hand shot up and stayed up. "Who here knows how to dance?" Once again, every hand rocketed to the sky. "How many of you are painters?" Yes, every hand rose, this time waving. There was just one difference between the two groups. The first was a group of lawyers, bankers, and corporate executives. The second was a group of first-graders.

As adults, we need to find a way to rekindle our youthful exuberance while maintaining a productive edge. Which is difficult in the business arena, considering the fragile nature of today's marketplace. Just think—at this very moment thousands of business meetings are in progress all around the world. And besides sharing important information, the number-one purpose for most of these meetings is to dissect problematic situations and find the answers to resolve the situation. Unfortunately, as we explained in our discussion of "Yes . . . And!" in chapter 6, the phrases most often heard during these meetings are:

Been there, . . . done that!

No!

Yes, but . . .

Yes, or . . .

How can you make your next manager's meeting more productive and at the same time more fun than a sandbox with two shovels and a super soaker? How can a family of four decide where to go on summer vacation without yelling, pouting, or taking Grandma's name in vain? In this chapter we will arm you with the creative ammunition to battle stagnation and resignation in meetings and give you the tools to turn the next "bored" meeting into an all-on-board meeting. Here are the keys:

- Give and take
- Explore and heighten
- Setting the scene

Partly Cloudy with a Chance of Brainstorms

Next to knowing when to seize an opportunity, the most important thing in life is to know when to forego an advantage.

—Benjamin Disraeli

GIVE AND TAKE

Give and take seems so simple. Conceptually, it is the flowing process of "giving focus" and "taking focus" in the scenes of your life. In practice, it is where we tend to lose our balance. Think back to the Al Gore–George W. Bush presidential debates. At the end of the first debate it became very apparent that the American people (those outside partisanism) took umbrage with Al Gore's "I need to have the last word" debating style; it cost him in all the public opinion polls. During the second debate, increasingly aware of this tendency, he did his best to bite his tongue. Why? Regardless of whether he felt justified to rebut, Gore knew one simple fact: Nobody likes a know-it-all! We didn't like 'em in high school. We don't like 'em at the condominium association gathering. And we certainly don't like 'em at the company monthly meeting. So, what if that know-it-all is you?

Thank goodness you purchased this book. Seriously, there are times when each of us could afford to listen a little more and contribute a little less. Not that we don't have great things to contribute. It's just that balance can prove more beneficial in the long run and having the right word is more important than having the last word.

Improvisers are extremely aware of the importance of not only verbal, but also physical, give and take. This includes battling the bad habit known as "upstaging." For improvisers, to upstage means to stand in a position on stage that forces fellow actors to stand with their backs to the audience just so they can face you. Can you think of anyone you work with or spend personal time with who tends to upstage people? What would constitute upstaging in a business meeting? Do any of these examples sound familiar?

- Anyone who always has to sit in the "good" chair or near the window.
- A person who spreads his or her stuff out on the table, taking up more space than anyone else.
- Someone who taps a pen continually and looks at his or her watch or sighs to show impatience.
- The person who constantly gets up and moves about while someone else is speaking.
- People who read, check voice mail, or hold separate conversations while someone else is speaking.

Each of these is an example of upstaging. These are selfish actions intended to draw attention or focus to the offending party. Upstagers are takers, not givers. In order for meetings to be effective, the actions of takers should not be condoned. Remember, it is important to share the physical stage of your life as well as the vocal stage. Focus on give and take. You will see how easy the exchange and transfer of great ideas and thoughts becomes. This will allow you the freedom to reclaim your childhood playfulness and boundless creativity. It can also lead to better business decisions and a more enjoyable work environment.

WHO WANTS TO PARTY?

Saturn, the automobile manufacturer, challenged their people to find a creative solution to this dilemma: "We need to find a way to thank the people who buy our cars. How can we show our appreciation, other than giving them a coupon good for a free oil change?" They wanted something different, something fresh, something people would remember . . . and they got it. A party! The reasoning? Parties are upbeat, fun, can be shared by the whole family (kids love balloons), and they embrace the idea of giving. You can't take a party, but you sure can give one!

EXPLORE AND HEIGHTEN

> Man's mind stretched to a new idea never goes back to its
> original dimensions.
> —Oliver Wendell Holmes

Once we've gotten a good handle on give and take, it's time to shift our meetings to the next level of creativity. The best way to accomplish this is through a technique known as "Explore and Heighten." The object of employing this technique at meetings is to expand the creative boundaries of those in attendance. It is only by pushing or stretching our boundaries or comfort zones to the level of absurdity that we find out what our acceptable limits are. That goes for both our business and personal lives. And sometimes, just sometimes, it is out there in the realm of the "What if?" that we find the key to our true potential.

IMPROVISE THIS!

YOU KNOW THE IMPROV DRILL

The Nickname Game

The goal of the following drill is to help you sharpen your "Explore and Heighten" muscles. This same drill can be expanded to serve larger groups as well. And it can be great family fun. But for now, it's just you . . . you, a dozen Krispy Kreme doughnuts, and a vivid imagination.

Step 1:

Find a place where there is a heavy flow of foot traffic. The local mall is always a great place. Situate yourself where people tend to slow for a bit or mill about before moving on. Next to portable kiosks or the mall directory are good spots.

Step 2:

Let your eyes scan the area. You needn't look closely at every person; you are truly waiting for inspiration. You are waiting and watching for someone in the crowd who, without even knowing it, demands your attention. It could be the rigid way they walk. It could be the stylish clothes they wear. It could be the wafting of perfume or cologne they emit as they pass. It could be a funky hat they don. It doesn't matter as long as it speaks to you.

Step 3:

Now focus your entire concentration on this person. Without overthinking, give this person a nickname. Go with your first impulse. To help you relax, remember this: There are no wrong answers. Whatever nickname you choose is great. Just let the nickname be inspired by that thing that stands out about this person.

If this person stands out because of a big thick beard and a wild tie-dyed T-shirt you may think to yourself: "It's sixties man!" Congratulations, you have just improvised in the truest form.

Step 4:
Now create a brief biography for this person. Or simply create a reason that this person is there. Let's continue with sixties man as our example. Maybe your creative mind ponders, "He has just put up black light posters everywhere and is looking for the big switch to turn off all the mall lights, expect the purple fluorescence. Cool, dude." Or maybe your thoughts are, "He once was a security guard for the Grateful Dead, now he's crafting wooden clogs by hand. Please welcome to *The Dating Game,* bachelor number two." It doesn't matter. Whatever your mind tells you is the story—hey, that's the story.

Step 5:
As sixties man moves on, let him go. Start scanning the area for your next creation. You may find that some of these characters come back through again and again. Go ahead, justify why they have returned. You may start to weave some of these people together in a story line. Fantastic!

Step 6:
Grab your journal. Jot down a few of the nickname creations that most moved you, for whatever reason. You never know when they could come in handy.

Like most things, you will find that by doing this improv drill a few times you will develop a keener sense and heightened awareness of the people around you. And without planning to do so you will find that in the most unlikely moments (fancy dinner party, business merger meeting, high school reunion) you will spot someone who is begging for a nickname. Go ahead, give yourself permission to play. We promise not to ground you.

Business as Unusual

We've explored Give and Take and Explore and Heighten as improvisation tools that can help us redirect our energies and put us on the path to greater creativity. How can we relate them directly to the workplace and, specifically, business meetings?

As we wrote in chapter 6, "Yes . . . And!" relates to our attitude. And in the world of business, even meetings have an attitude. The problem is, the attitude of most meetings is rarely conducive to forward thinking and creativity as a means to reach an end. They are most often dry, repetitious, mundane, and predictable. And the last thing anyone or any business wants to be is predictable. Reliable? Yes. Consistent? Yes. Predictable? No! And yet common sense should tell us that if the one thing we do more than any other (hold meetings) is predictable, predictability will become the pervasive attitude of our existence.

YOU KNOW THE IMPROV DRILL

Please Pass the Pumpkin

One of the best exercises for developing effective give and take is "Please Pass the Pumpkin." Here's how it works. Whoever is first to speak at a meeting holds (in this case) a softball sized toy pumpkin. When they finish speaking, if someone wishes to reply or comment, they must raise their hand. The pumpkin is dropped, both the person who threw it and the person attempting to catch it are silenced. That is, they cannot participate verbally in the meeting at this point. Instead, they become note takers for the meeting. So, how long are these two silenced? Well, it all depends. They must continue their task as preeminent note-takers until someone *else* drops the pumpkin. At that time our first two are replaced (as note-takers) by the two people who currently mishandled the pumpkin, and may now re-join the game. *Note: When the pumpkin is dropped, the person who dropped it must pick it up and hand it to the person on their immediate left. That person then makes a positive declaration about the person who just handed them the pumpkin. Then off we go again—the meeting continues.*

Here's why we like this exercise:

1. It encourages people to work together on a project.
2. People must make solid eye contact. Communication is key.
3. It supports the concept that rarely is a mistake the fault or responsibility of just one person.
4. It makes one really check in before speaking, or even asking to speak. Is what you want to say really that important?
5. It increases energy in the room and between people.
6. It's fun and leads to creative explosions.

Two points of practicality—

a. If it proves too easy for everyone to catch the pumpkin, only allow the use of one hand—the person's nondominant hand.
b. In no way is this exercise intended to stifle our creative, go-from-the-gut improv urges. It is only intended to heighten our awareness of the importance of give and take and active listening in a meeting scenario or group setting. Once you've sharpened your skill level you can truly unleash your creative spontaneity. Remember—small steps.

SETTING THE SCENE

Remember, the goal here is to find a way to make meetings more productive by challenging your team, staff, or family to tap into their creative ingenuity and turn their backs on traditional thinking. We firmly believe that, like all good improvisers, you only need encouragement and a nurturing environment to access your "child's mind."

In what ways can your workspace become a nurturing environment? What elements can be included to lighten the mood and heighten the 'tude? Keep these questions in mind as we close out chapter 8 by looking at ways you can reshape your meetings and your thoughts about meetings to make them more productive and a wellspring of creativity.

TIPS ON THE TOPIC

- Instead of a memo (**m**ildly **e**ffective, **m**ostly **o**verrated) announce the next meeting by typing a poem on a piece of paper, fashioning it like a paper airplane, and flying it into people's offices. A poem? How about . . .

> *At eleven o'clock this fair Monday*
> *Tell all you come across*
> *We shall convene in the conference room*
> *I'll see you there . . . The Boss*

- Change the location of meetings occasionally. This will help give everyone a fresh outlook by changing the stimuli of your environment. Nothing like a lunch meeting on the rooftop to accentuate the concept of expansive thinking to the troops.

- Start each meeting with a group exercise. Something to get everyone out of his or her premeeting mindset and into a new group mindset.

- Once everyone is finally seated, get everyone back up and reseat them using some unique method. Maybe, alphabetically by state of birth? This not only shakes up set seating patterns, but it also offers the chance to share a little information about the individuals that they might not have shared previously. When two people find out they are both from the great state of Vermont, a new door of communication is opened and a bond is formed.

- Have different people organize and set the agenda for upcoming meetings. This will give everyone a stronger sense of involvement and help develop their leadership skills. Try it with your children and watch them rise to the occasion.

- Find a way to include music. People respond to music. It inspires energy and puts people in a like frame of mind. Ask people to bring in a CD that includes their favorite song. When things start to grind down in a meeting, pop in the CD and crank it up, even if just for thirty seconds. The change will do you good.

- Each meeting should have at least one element of *play*. This will help keep everyone in touch with his or her creative side. We are particularly fond of the mid-meeting break for graham crackers and cappuccinos, a perfect complement to "show and tell," where the vice president of sales enlightens us about his new Ping putter.

PERSONAL EXERCISE 8
String-a-Song-Along

The Players: You, and your vocal gymnastics.

The Object: To seed the clouds of your personal brainstorming abilities through "Explore and Heighten," becoming an in-the-moment spontaneous singer/songwriter.

How To: **Singer:** Find a quiet place, one that's preferably soundproof. A padded cell will do in a pinch. Why? Because you're about to sing your lungs out. A capella. Now, pick up a newspaper, and turn it to any page. Take a deep breath, and choose the first word you eyes fall upon.

Immediately begin singing a song based upon your chosen word. Any song. That's right. Make it up! Let's say for example the word was "power." If the first song that pops into your mind is Huey Lewis's "Power of Love," sing it continuously until a key word in that song pops into your psyche.

Let's say it's "love." Now flow into a song with the word "love" in it. Suddenly you're Barbra Streisand singing, "Love, soft as an easy chair . . . Love, fresh as the morning air . . ." Another key word—"morning"—presents itself to you. Presto. You're Cat Stevens wailing, "Morning has broken, like the first morning . . ." Got the flow? Continue on as far as you can take it. More words, more songs until you've created an instant top-forty medley. (It doesn't have to be golden oldies. But caution: Stay clear of Italian operas.)

Ready for the advanced version?

Songwriter: Repeat the above exercise, except improvise original songs—lyrics and melody.

Hints: As in all of our exercises, commit fully to the process—after each medley, give yourself a quick pep talk and begin another one. Remember to heighten your emotion with each song. "Getting into it" is by far the easiest way to get out of your head and into the spirit of this game.

The Result: With plenty of repetition, you'll feel increased comfort and confidence in your personal on-the-spot brainstorming ability. And singing in the shower will take on a whole new dimension.

NINE

SPEAKING OF SPEAKERS

Are You a Woofer or a Tweeter?

A speech should not just be a sharing of information,
but a sharing of yourself.
—Ralph Archbold

Whether you've given several hundred speeches or you can't muster the courage to give your son's pet fish a eulogy over the toilet, adding improvisation techniques to your repertoire will help you overcome anxiety, think on your feet, and receive wild cheers and rounds of applause.

And All That Jazz

The best improvisers have studied and learned their craft and the best jazz musicians understand the basics of jazz. Jazz musicians improvise around a melody line, going off on riffs, but always returning to the theme of the piece. Once they've mastered the basics they can stray and stretch their creative muscles. The same is true for comedians, humorists, improvisers, and speakers. We have learned over the years that consistently working toward your goals, a little bit each day, and focusing on one thing that will get you closer to where you want to be will enable you to reach your goal. Take the movie *Groundhog Day* starring Bill Murray, as an example. Give the guy a little time and he can speak French and create ice sculptures. And yes, get slapped a lot. That happens when you're learning. So, plan on getting slapped along the way. (In the end, you get the girl!)

We're going to address four main concepts in this chapter that will help you move through your nervousness, connect with your audiences, and have some fun.

- Make the connection
- Spontaneity
- Storytelling

It Could Happen

Recently the CEO of a major insurance company addressed his company at the annual staff meeting. The plan was for the audience to walk away with the feeling that their stuffy yet compassionate leader had finally departed from his usual canned speech. He'd look them in the eye and speak from his heart. He tossed his Armani jacket over the podium and rolled up his sleeves. It was clear that this time he would speak with passion on his company and his commitment to each and every person in the audience. "I want to tell you a personal story about a little boy working at a hot dog stand . . . and a dream." Tears welled up in his eyes. "That little boy was m—" At that precise moment the TelePrompTer went blank—as did this CEO's brain. He lost his place in his speech. The audience stared at him; he stared at his executive assistant, who looked at the AV person, who looked out the window.

Maybe you connected with that story because you've been in that CEO's place. Or, God forbid, you were the AV person. We've all experienced a moment where a script would have been really handy. Everyone can speak in public. Everyone can improvise. Everyone can learn what he or she chooses to learn. Choosing to be more spontaneous on the platform (a necessity when AV equipment takes a nap) is just that. A choice. And a little work.

Let's say for the sake of this book that you've made that choice. First, we'd like to compliment you on a fine decision. The difference between a good speaker and a great speaker is in how you connect with the audience. If the CEO in the above story was giving a heartfelt speech and connected to his audience, he could have improvised and pulled out experiences from his past. Or at least someone's past. Expect the unexpected. And when you really get comfortable, you'll embrace the unexpected!

MAKE THE CONNECTION

In order to be spontaneous you need to trust yourself and be totally open to your environment, intellectually, physically, and intuitively. By tapping into your intuition you can do nothing else but respond in the immediacy, the now. It is at this moment when you possess the gift of being totally yourself that you will connect with your audience in a way delivering a verbatim, written speech cannot. It is also at that moment when most people get nervous and want to throw up.

To understand that you are there for your audience is the single most important thing you can do. It's akin to the wise advice given to people who are depressed. If you focus on someone who needs help more than you do, you won't focus on yourself so much. This may come as a surprise, but it's not about you! It's not about you looking stupid or receiving a standing ovation. It's about sharing what you have to share with the audience in a way that will keep their attention, teach them something, or amuse them. However, if you're at a point where simply keeping them from nodding off and sliding down their chair into REM sleep is your primary concern, perhaps a Dale Carnegie course is in your future.

Most successful speakers practice what they want to say, and when things don't go perfectly—and they seldom do—they are prepared. So, know your material. Trust you can rely on your own knowledge and your connection with the audience to get you through it. Notice, we didn't say, know your speech verbatim and don't miss a beat. (Unless you're the president. And if you are the president and you're reading this book, could you please endorse it for the next printing? Get back to us.) We said *know* your material. Write out your draft verbatim, know what you want to say, and then write it out as bullet points.

Here's Why . . . If the CEO Story Didn't Convince You

Ever get a call from the phone company trying to sell you long-distance services? If you answered no to this question you're probably living in Montana writing a manifesto in between reading these chapters. Okay, so the phone company calls and goes through their litany of questions and you dare throw in a question of your own. They go completely berserk. They've lost their place and don't have a clue what to say next. Why? Because they don't know their subject. Try this sometime for fun.

Knowing your material will also help you with stage fright. The more you know the more in control you feel. And it allows you to be spontaneous with your knowledge. Here's an example. A true story.

Miss Malaprop

Molly was giving a speech on networking at a dinner to a prestigious college alumni association. As she often does, she quoted Woody Allen's line, "Ninety percent of success is showing up." Although, when she said it, the words came out, "Ninety percent of sex is showing up." The audience roared. You may be thinking, "Oh, how awful!" But it was truly an unplanned gift. After correcting herself, she referred to the misquote and said, "Well, at least that's what my husband says." And got a double laugh. Because she connected with her audience and knew her material, she could go "off script," have some fun and come right back to her topic.

The Human Factor

This brings us to a very serious matter. The use of humor. Chapter 7 taught us how important it was in our lives. Well, it's equally important on the platform. There's an old joke that goes: Do I have to use humor in my speeches? Only if you want to get paid or only if you want the audience to remember anything. Humor relaxes people. Laughing releases those great endorphins. Free drugs, ya gotta love that. And laughing will relax you too! On the spot, audience participation humor is always welcome and almost always successful. This kind of humor does not involve a red clown nose or an arrow through your head—although, if you could get one to actually go through your head, by all means, go for it.

You're going to be able to tap into this sort of humor if you're there—physically, mentally there. Tapping into your audience alerts you to people dozing off or starting a game of gin rummy in the back. You aren't reading your speech, you're looking at them. You're comfortable with who you are. Your reaction to the audience makes your presentation spark and shows them your speech is not canned.

> What I want people to do is laugh so
> they see things seriously.
> —William R. Zinner

Consider Julia Roberts's spontaneous Screen Actors Guild acceptance speech. She walked to the podium, threw her head back, genuinely laughed, and said, "You really have to take notice of anything the Screen Actors Guild does for a woman." Her spontaneous sarcasm sent the audience into peals of laughter. She said, "It just came to me when I was actually holding the award." She was so comfortable with who she was, she could say what she was thinking. And that usually works.

It helps if you have a sense of humor (the same thing has been said about marriage . . .). But don't worry if you're no Bill Cosby, there are lots of resources to help you learn the mechanics of humor.

There's so much to learn about the use of humor in a presentation. You need to know what's appropriate and what isn't. Like a gun, you should never point it at others when it's loaded. Unless you're Don Rickles or George Carlin, it's going to serve you better to make fun of yourself rather than others. Self-deprecating humor endears you to your audience and makes you seem more approachable. But be careful, if you're a five-foot, six-inch woman who weighs 116 pounds, no matter how fat you feel you are not going to get weight joke laughs. You would lose your audience faster than Oprah could down a Slim Fast shake. Overweight people can make fat jokes. Bald people can make bald jokes. You get the idea.

Humor has unique benefits. It connects you to your audience, reduces stress and it can make people physically feel better. But it can also make people very uncomfortable and even be hurtful. When you are up in front of people it is your responsibility to use humor wisely. With a few simple guidelines, you'll find the appropriate use of humor will make you a much sought after presenter.

SPONTANEITY

In gathering interviews for her book, *What to Say When You're Dying on the Platform,* author Lily Walters references speakers who use what on the surface appear to be ad-libbed responses, but in actuality are planned or predetermined responses to situations that may arise. Her book cites two great examples of what speakers have at the ready for that unique moment when an audience member passes gas. Terry Paulson, past president of the National Speakers Association, when met with this gaseous hurdle calmly responded, "Well, that brings us to the subject of nonverbal communication." And noted speaker Tom Ogden countered with the appropriate, "Critics!"

Although both are inherently valuable, it is important to distinguish the difference. It is important to note that the first time Tom Ogden said "critics" it was pure improvisation. Each subsequent time it was a planned response delivered with good comic timing. Simply put, an improvised response is not preplanned and therefore is truly original. A planned response is tried and true and, when well placed, is almost guaranteed to garner huge responses. What these two do have in common is that both require the speaker to be fully engaged in the moment and connected to the audience. Without this connection the golden opportunity for any response will most certainly be missed. And any speaker worth his or her salt will take note of an improvised remark that hit big the first time, catalog it, and dust it off for use at a later date with the seeming originality of Donna Karan's fall line of fashion.

One way to help you more readily recognize the potential moments to include planned comments is to observe other speakers. Analyze their delivery, pick their speech apart, look for those times when they evoked humorous responses, and then ask yourself, Why did that work? What was it that made that funny? Chances are it involved some classic, foolproof quips that brought the house down.

Toast of the Town

Anyone asked to give a toast at the spur of the moment is bound to feel a little nervous. Just before stepping in front of the microphone to give a toast (which is tantamount to the average person stepping through the velvet curtain into a sea of blinding lights on a Broadway stage), panic may creep in. That heart pounding, sweaty palms, "I would rather eat Kibbles and Bits for the next week than do this" feeling. You ask yourself, what should I say to these people? Relax. They're probably all oiled up anyway. Nervousness is okay. In fact it can provide that needed adrenaline rush that gives you energy. Panic isn't okay though. So, here are a few suggestions to help you the next time you're asked to speak on the spot, and for those times when you know you'll be called upon to dazzle people with your wit and heart.

When you first stand up in front of your audience:

- Receive their support. Connect with them.
- Be still for a moment before you begin and look around at the friendly faces.
- Begin speaking from your heart instead of your head. When you are willing to be yourself, even though you may not think that's what a speaker should do, you become magnetic.
- Let your words flow from your relationship to the person you're toasting. Drop the barrier between you (the speaker) and them (the audience), and connect with them as individuals.

We expect you know what we mean and won't go too far.

> Women, can't live with 'em . . . pass the beer nuts.
> —Norm Peterson, wedding toast scene, *Cheers*

Norm did exactly what we said. But the result wasn't exactly what we were looking for. Go back to the well and fill yourself with some information before you attend the event. In a moment of creative inspiration, write something just for the occasion.

Let's say you are going to give a wedding toast to your good friends, B and Mike. Everyone knows Mike loves golf and B likes to shop:

Here's to you both
A beautiful pair
On your wedding and your love affair
"B" and Mike, each other you adore
So give each other room
To shop and golf more!

Once you have something—a nugget to get you started—trust yourself. Trust your relationship and your history with people. Good toasts come from tapping into the heart of a relationship. Believe in yourself. Jean-Paul Sartre once said, "You are your choices." So, today's assignment is to write something for someone. Kick start yourself. Remember, the learning is in the doing.

Presentations—They Couldn't Have Planned That!

We teach improvisation, so the last thing we want to do is give a canned presentation. In order to pick up material, we always arrive early to watch the speaker before us. It never fails—we are given plenty to use in our own program just by watching and listening. And we never know where the new information will present itself. Case in point: We did a sales program for the Rainforest Café. The first speaker did two different bits where he asked the audience for a five dollar bill. He always gave them back and went on with his program. Although we rehearsed our opening, we knew this was a gift.

We incorporated his material into our opening by jumping on stage and saying, "Who's got a twenty dollar bill?" Which got a huge laugh. We took the twenty, making the point: You never know what you can get unless you ask for it. The perfect opening for a sales presentation. And yes, yes . . . we gave it back. Know your material, but listen for gems of information that you can add—on the spot!

Now, what made the twenty dollar bill bit funny was that everyone in the room was in on it together. If you're completely wigged out and maniacally going over your speech verbatim you wouldn't be open to new information. It would throw you. If you are in the moment and open to people's "gifts," your presentation can take on new twists and you can flow with the audience's reactions to your program. So, pay attention. You might learn something. John F. Kennedy once said, "There are three things which are real: God, human folly, and laughter. The first two are beyond our comprehension. So we must do what we can with the third." So, let's.

Let's say you're going to give a presentation to the custodial staff at the Association of High School Principals. The first question you should ask yourself is, What do I want to say? You need to have a crystal clear vision about your purpose. You can't just show up and be funny. Well, you could and you would probably get asked back—but let's go deeper and say you're there to "communicate a message." Feeling comfortable and in the moment and confident in your material puts you in the best place to communicate the message. You're freeing yourself from nervous, self-conscious behavior. Don't make the audience "feel your pain." Have a plan to relieve nervous tension.

Improv Meets Jack La Lanne

Some improv actors do warm-ups before going on stage to do a show. And you should do some too before giving your speech in your life-scene. These should be activities that get your blood pumping and get you out of your head, clearing your mind of thoughts and of planning what you want to say, and allowing yourself to connect with the audience and feel confident.

YOU KNOW THE IMPROV DRILL

Let's Get Physical

Do something physical, such as jumping jacks. Move your mouth around in different shapes. Sing the scales. Take a brisk walk. S-t-r-e-t-c-h. Now, as improvisers do before a show, walk the space; feel the space. Know where the steps are to get on the stage. Go to the back of the room and take it in from that perspective. Move around the space as though you own it. It's yours. Check the AV equipment, your PowerPoint, the lighting. An audience wants you to be comfortable and relaxed on the platform. Moving around to get your blood pumping and knowing everything is in working order will help relieve tension and free you to be yourself.

STORYTELLING

When the Stories Flow . . . the Notes Will Go

Although we have been talking about spontaneity and planned responses while speaking, it is equally important to have prepared material, in the form of stories. Storytelling is one of the oldest forms of communication. It has maintained its place throughout the centuries by helping the speaker connect with the audience. Learning improvisation techniques, using the exercises in this book, will help you to become a better storyteller.

Although it seems that certain people are born with this talent and some are innately more skilled than others, storytelling is not just a gift. It's a learned skill. The speaker who gives a one-hour keynote relies on the power of stories to convey information, keep the audience emotionally involved, and stay on track without looking at notes. There is nothing worse than listening to a speaker read a presentation. (Unless it's a speaker who eats while reading his presentation.) Stories are a lot easier to remember than a full hour of facts and quotes. (And a lot more interesting.) Knowing a few great stories will free you from your notes. A professional speaker's typical outline may end up on a 4 x 6 card and look like this:

- Child story/opening
- Creativity facts
- South America kidnapping story
- Overheads
- Voicemail story
- Dr. Seuss poem
- Additional info if needed: Coin story. Reagan quote. Group pencil activity.

Now, doesn't that look a lot less cumbersome than a twelve-page speech written verbatim? No turning pages, no losing your place, and the audience doesn't even know you're looking at notes because it only takes a one-second glance. You don't have to worry about going in a different direction or not getting it perfect because you haven't memorized your speech word for word. It gives you a lot of room to be spontaneous and room to improvise, knowing that you will somehow get back on track. Okay. You want to know how you can get to the point where you can write your presentation in bullet points?

- Make an outline of the content areas you want to cover and write out each section on a sheet of paper. You can also do this by writing each section on large Post-It notes and then arranging them on the wall.
- Take concepts that go together and put them in one area, another concept in another area and so on. Once you have them in their respective sections, arrange them in a row so you can visually see the flow of your speech. You will get a feel for its order. In this practice you will also see where your speech needs energy; many times this will be the place you'll put a story. Or, you can make a point, tell a story, make a point, tell a story. The story is the real-life application of your point.
- Stand back and look at the flow. Does it make sense? Will it keep the audience's attention? Should you give it up and go pump gas?

In your quest for the perfect story, remember that, as important as it is to have a great story, it takes skill to tell it. Listen to recordings of articulate speakers, play them over and over and pay attention to nuances. The speakers will raise and lower their voices, inflect vowel sounds up and down, and use silence as a powerful attention grabber. You can purchase these tapes from the National Speakers Association (www.nsaspeaker.org; 480-968-0911).

Act It Out!

A great story can be enhanced by the use of miming actions within the story. (Watch an actor tell a story on *The Tonight*

Show with Jay Leno—they will act out the entire thing.) It makes it much more entertaining to listen to. Remember the exercise when you opened a present, and you felt it and could see its colors? Or the exercise when you opened the cupboard and took out a glass of water and you held the glass? Those exercises will help you tell stories more colorfully. If you have a pregnant woman in your story—act her out: waddle like her, sigh like her. If there's a man smoking a cigar in your story, take time to act out what it feels like, then mime that part in your story. Rehearse your stories, know a few quotes, have a few standard lines, and practice.

Storytelling does take practice. It takes paying attention to details and noticing your surroundings. A great exercise to help you with storytelling is to sit at an airport, the state fair, or the mall. (You may have noticed we do a lot of mall observations . . .) Watch people and describe what they look like. Every detail—how they smell, walk, and talk. Exactly how is that cigarette hanging off that woman's chapped lower lip? What is that man doing? Exactly what mannerisms make my mother-in-law so annoying? It's best to do this in your head— to avoid getting punched.

Gathering Stories

Paying attention will jump-start your ability to take in the world and notice things. It will spark your senses. Your life is full of stories you can apply to your presentations—but, you have to pay attention. Use your journal, carry it with you everywhere and write down experiences and ideas you have. Hear something funny? Write it down. See something strange? Write it down. Observe life. It's all a story.

As you perfect your speaking skills, strive to make connec-

tions with your audience. Perfecting a presentation takes anywhere from one week to twenty-five years. It's a journey, a
process. As you grow, you will delight in your talents and your
ability to communicate a message in a unique and highly authentic way. You will develop your own style and confidence.
No one can give a presentation, a toast, or a speech like you.
Because no one observes the world exactly like you do. They
don't have your unique slant—and that's what you bring to an
audience.

When There's a "Will," There's a Way

Will Rogers, arguably one of the best and most famous
speakers, was a wonderful storyteller. He said, "ah" and "um"
a lot. He wasn't polished and didn't look the part. He would
have been thrown out of Toastmasters faster than a flying
tomato. And yet he was considered a true talent. He could
hold an audience's attention because he was authentic and
had something interesting to say. People listening to Will
Rogers didn't drop a mental marble into a jar every time he
said "um" or used hand gestures that weren't Toastmasters-
appropriate.

Florence Littauer, Certified Speaking Professional (this title
just begs the question, Are you required to be certified to
speak?), said, "We don't need to be afraid when we have mas-
tery of our material. Confidence can simply be a matter of experience." Like anything else, if you are going to do it once a
year—golf, write, improvise, speak—you're going to be a little
rusty each time you do it, so get experience by volunteering to
speak at church, the rotary, or Mom and Dad's career day at
school. The more you speak in public, the easier it gets. The
easier it gets, the more fun it is!

TIPS ON THE TOPIC

- Trust yourself! Be open to the scene, the environment: intellectually, physically, and intuitively.
- Prepare by learning your material. Read it as though you are learning information, not memorizing a speech.
- Act out your stories to add spice to your speech.
- Speak from your heart instead of your head.
- Use humor to relieve stress and connect to your audience.

PERSONAL EXERCISE 9
Ask Me Anything!

The Players: You!

The Object: To learn your material inside and out. Backward and forward. Twisted and turned and upside down—with you coming out on top.

How To: Get a stack of 4 × 6 index cards, preferably in varying colors, a black Flair marker, and some colorful bold markers. Using the black Flair markers, write out questions using the bullet points of your speech. For instance, one card might say, "I begin my speech with what quote?" Another might say, "Why is leadership so important to a successful business?" Write out the questions as though you're a teacher writing a test. (C'mon, you know you've always wanted to be on that side of the desk.)

Speaking of Speakers

Next, take your bright and beautiful colored markers and write out how you're going to answer the questions. Suggestions:

1. In an Irish accent

2. As Dr. Evil from *The Spy Who Shagged Me*

3. In an English accent

4. With contempt

5. As Bart from *The Simpsons*

6. As a six-year-old

7. As Shaggy from *Scooby Doo*

After blowing off your linear thinking cap add some of your own.

Now, find a large room where you have space to walk around. Take the deck of index cards with the questions written on them and hold them over your head and drop them; watch them sail to the ground. Pick up just one card and answer the question as though you are in a Q and A session after your speech. Don't look at notes unless you have gone completely brain dead.

When you've mastered all the cards, go to the advanced version. Pick up all the cards and shuffle them. Throw them over your head, and then pick up one card from each pile. Answer the question in the format the colorful marker cards suggest.

The Result: Complete and utter knowledge of your speech. You will now have the confidence to go "off script" and come back to your speech without the fear of forgetting something. And here's a bonus: You've improvised characters, dialects, and styles, which will help you add depth and personality to your stories.

AN INSIDE TIP FROM OUTSIDE THE BOX

DALE IRVIN

Professional Speaker

Dale Irvin is a professional speaker. He holds the distinction of being a Certified Speaking Professional (CSP) and has received the Council of Peers Award of Excellence (CPAE). He grew up in Cleveland then moved to Chicago to go into the advertising business. He uses improvisation as the benchmark to his speeches, training, and his trademark "five-minute funnies," where Dale recaps convention and meeting highlights at the event's general sessions.

Q: Dale, what was your first introduction to improvisation?

A: *I moved to Chicago to go into the ad business, but I really wanted to perform. I saw an ad for a local theater and tried out. I was surprisingly cast as the lead. Surprisingly, in that I knew nothing about acting. I thought I'd better learn fast so I took classes at the Second City Player's Workshop.*

Q: What was it like?

A: *It was a phenomenal experience. I was rather shy and improv was the perfect tool for me. It helped me gain confidence. I was slightly intimidated because, well, those people ain't right. The experience completely changed the way I looked at things—my perspective changed. It must have made an impact on me because when it was over I formed an improv troupe. Then went into stand-up.*

Q: So, how did you get into speaking?

A: *My stand-up act went from five minutes to thirty minutes and pretty soon I built up an act and then a speech. Then I discovered that associations and corporations pay a lot more when you have content. I learned about all the positive benefits of humor and laughter—and that became the message people would pay for.*

Q: How could others use it to enhance their speaking?

A: *One obvious way it can help a speaker is with "thinking on your feet." With any performance, speech, or presentation something can go wrong. The microphone goes out, a tray of dishes crashes to the floor—being skilled at improv allows you to come up with a comment that will get the attention back onto you, where it belongs, and off of the disturbance. It prepares you for the unexpected. And it sure couldn't hurt our politicians.*

Q: How so?

A: *Being "in the moment" makes people more real. Look at Bob Dole, he knows how to improvise but chose not to. Bad move. In real life no one holds a conversation like politicians do. It just makes people seem more real when they have the ability to take in what's happening around them and react in the moment. Bill Clinton improvised—mostly to pick up chicks. Then there's the nemesis of improvisation: Al Gore.*

Q: What would you be doing if you never learned to improvise?

A: *Well, I've still got contacts at my old paper route . . .*

Q: How about a final tip for our readers, Dale?

A: *First of all, improvisation can help* everyone. *It's just a great skill. Take time to observe life, make insightful comments and stark realizations. It teaches you to just look around you—and not so you don't trip but to observe things. To look at life from different angles. It's a process and you file the information in your mind. You never know when you're going to use it.*

TEN

THROW AWAY THE SCRIPT!

How to Improv(e) Your Customer Service

Why not go out on the limb? Isn't that where the fruit is?

—Frank Scully

When an automobile's gas tank is empty, that is a bad thing. When a joint checking account is empty, that is even worse. But, when an improviser is empty, it is a glorious thing to behold. Everyday, in classes around the world, improvisers are asked to "throw away the script" and get empty. Yes, you're right, improvisers don't use a script. Still, they must rid themselves of preconceived notions and expectations and embrace the idea that not knowing what is about to happen next is exactly where they need to be.

The best improvisers are not actors . . . they are re-actors.

Unfortunately, in the business world, the opposite approach to throwing away the script is often encouraged and promoted. Many owners, supervisors, and line managers believe that the best way to deal with customers or guests is to treat them all in the exact same manner—to develop standardized greetings, fairly stock answers to all questions, and absolute uniformity across all corporate lines.

In physics, this works: "For every action there is an opposite and equal reaction." In customer service, it works better like this: "For every action there should be a reaction, it needn't be opposite or equal, but it damn well better be appropriate!"

Now please understand, we truly believe in and applaud preparation and consistency. The Ritz Carlton is the Ritz Carlton for one reason: They provide spectacular service. But, they also realize that you must leave room for the unexpected. They understand that sometimes all of the knowledge in the world will not solve certain problems. Therefore, they empower their employees to deal with the guests, listen to their concerns and needs, and then proceed to bring about satisfactory resolution in hopes of exceeding the guest's expectations. Only by being empty, by understanding that there isn't a script for every situation, can this be accomplished.

There is a phrase that actors often use to convey the idea that their performance on any given night was staid, uninspired, and halfhearted: "I phoned that one in." The implication? Although they were physically present, in every other capacity they were AWOL. They did nothing more than go through the motions. Have you ever just phoned it in?

> ### GO AHEAD . . . ANSWER IT!
>
> Take a Post-It note and on it write, "Throw Away the Script." Now each and every time someone calls, after you have greeted them and you are into the "next level" of the conversation, "throw away the script," and react to that person, that conversation, "in the moment." Don't fall back on your standard lines; say something appropriate based on what the person said to you. Add a twist, some humor, empathy, whatever the situation calls for. It will make it more fun and interesting for you and the caller.

In our efforts to help you "throw away the script" we will focus on three areas where an improvisational touch can truly enhance your customer service.

- Learn it—then burn it
- Fast-acting and long-lasting relationships
- Take a moment to make a moment

Before we boldly step off the safe confines of the service curb into oncoming customer traffic, let's look at how being "in the moment" at just the right moment can change everything.

How 'bout a little Personality?

Kathy, a woman who works out of her home in order to be with her children, was doing a transaction with a bank representative on the phone. It was the usual drill: "What's your account number?" "Your mother's maiden name?" "Your social security number?" "PIN number?" As Kathy was frantically digging for the information her son stepped forward and proudly displayed his latest attempt to write his name. "That's wonderful! You can use a pencil!" Kathy exclaimed. The service rep (knowing Kathy was talking to her son) said, "Thank you, but *actually* I've been using one for a long time now." Kathy laughed out loud and suddenly (funny how this works) felt like her bank was more than a four-story brick building.

LEARN IT . . . THEN BURN IT

As you can see, based on Kathy's story, somewhere between *Stepford* service (the land of perpetual rigidity—where every word, movement, and action is accounted for, leaving no room for spontaneity) and total chaos or "Three Stooges" service (the land of eternal ineptitude) is where the most productive organizations thrive. They realize the importance of entrusting to their staffs the monumental task of being real, making the company they work for a living, breathing, and feeling entity. They also realize that they cannot send their staffs out to face the masses ill equipped. They train them well and then do what all good parents do: Up their allowance and allow them to think for themselves.

Practical Makes Perfect

Practical is good. We're not sure how it became attached to jokes, as in *practical* jokes, but it does pay to be practical. However, there is no law that says that you must become inflexible, rigid, or unmovable in order to be practical. Take Southwest Airlines. (Nuts! We didn't want to use them as an example again. If another company could do it like they do, we'd use them.) They realize the importance and practicality of going through preflight safety instructions for their passengers. They also realize that most people have flown before and therefore have heard these instructions at some point in time. Southwest empowers their flight attendants to just learn it—then burn it. They are encouraged to give the instructions their own twist. Hence: "If you are seated next to a child . . . or someone acting like a child, put your own oxygen mask on first." Or "If you are connecting on another Southwest flight, agents at the gate will be happy to assist you. If your connecting flight is on another airline . . . we really don't care." Or "The use of cellular phones is prohibited. As is the use of Karaoke machines."

As you can see, practicality is prudent. But it needn't be prudish. This is especially true in what we call face companies. These are companies where face-to-face interactions occur. It only takes a second to know whether the person you are dealing with is actually present and available to communicate, and it happens before they ever open their mouths. It's nonverbal communication and it starts with the face: It starts with a smile.

C'mon . . . Smile

Julia Roberts is by all Hollywood assessments an attractive woman. Of course, there are times when she is less attractive and times when she is more. But, when she smiles she lights up more homes than a California power company. She becomes radiant. She immediately becomes more accessible and we are drawn to her like moths to the flame. It is the one of the reasons she has done picture after picture after picture. Compare her to the Mona Lisa—who offered nothing but that tight-lipped, uninviting, and repellent smirk. And what did she do? One picture? Enough said.

Take the time to smile. It's better than a business card. And remember, we can't see your smile if your head is in your script.

Just like the improviser who learns the principles and techniques of improvisation and then steps on stage with nothing but a pocketful of confidence, or the golfer who on the driving range goes through his or her mental checklist from a countless number of lessons, then leaves the checklist there on the way to the first tee, you can prepare yourself so there is nothing unnerving about the unknown as you take the customer service stage.

FAST-ACTING AND LONG-LASTING RELATIONSHIPS

We all know that good products are essential to the fiscal stability of any business. But good products are not enough. Today's corporate climate, coupled with consumers yearning for service and an "experience," tells us that relationships are the linchpin to continuing growth, customer loyalty, and long-term profitability.

Think for a moment about the various places of business that you frequent on a regular basis. Now try to separate them into two distinct categories. The first we'll call the product businesses and the second we'll refer to as the human factor–based businesses. The first category might include the phone company, the electric company, your triple-platinum, frequent-flier credit card company, the self-service, pay-at-the-pump gas station; businesses that are product- or services-driven and where a face or name is rarely associated with the services rendered.

Overwhelmingly, our choices about product-based businesses come down to savings and proximity (i.e., if you're closer and cheaper, we're in business). But our choices about human factor–based businesses aren't as cut and dried. In the ever-changing world of customer service one thing remains a constant. Like improvisation scenes, the businesses that flourish are the ones based on strong relationships, externally and internally.

First Impressions

All relationships start with first impressions. And they are either good or they're bad. When customers have a good impression of you, they also have a good impression of your company. Think of it this way: Whenever you interact with a customer they fill out a mental comment card. Every time the customer deals with your business a new impression is left. The moment a customer first sets foot into a restaurant; when the sales associate presents the purchase receipt; when the dentist sits down with the patient to discuss treatment—these are all impression points. And they can strengthen the image of your company or come back to bite you in your assets.

The department of motor vehicles, an unlikely place to witness a stellar service transaction, made a wonderful impression on one of our workshop attendees. She shared this story.

Recently I went in to get a new license. There were two lines offering distinctly different service. Servicing one line was a middle-aged, battle-ax woman, cranking people along like she was working in a factory. She was toxic. ("Have your picture ID ready. *Next!*") Heading up the other line was another middle-aged woman sporting a smile and gaining eye contact with everyone, whether you were next in line or fifth in line. Needless to say, I chose her line. I told her I needed a new license and she said, "And we're going to make sure we get that pretty necklace in your photo!" She took her time setting up the photo, and made sure I was smiling. She paid attention, was in the moment, and created a favorable impression. Unlike her colleague, who offered a robotized, impersonal transaction. I love my license photo! And I think of that woman every time I cash a check.

Check in with yourself, especially at the end of the day. Take a few minutes to review your interactions with customers. Did you create favorable impressions and treat each interaction as a new "customer scene"? Did you seize opportunities to improvise with people and have fun? What went well? What should you have been fired for? Most important of all, what could have been done better?

TAKE A MOMENT TO MAKE A MOMENT

> At the heart of effective leadership is genuinely
> caring for people.
> —James M. Kouzes and Barry Z. Posner, *Encouraging the Heart*

At the heart of joyously improvising your merry way through your personal and career life is developing the ability to recognize the appearance of golden moments: chance moments of opportunity where you face a choice to care enough about someone, in a personal or in a work relationship, to make an instant effort to go the extra mile, to make someone's day. (Okay, in the *positive* sense of "making someone's day" of course, not in the *Dirty Harry* threat or candidate Ronald Reagan's bluster.) You have the choice to either take a moment to make a moment or to allow that moment to slip away.

Many companies, large and small, have adopted this ultimate guest-service practice. Paris–Las Vegas Resort calls them "Extra Mile Moments." The storied Pike Place Fish Market, which has become a national training model for fun, focused, and playful customer service, calls the concept "Make Their Day." Guest Service wizards at Disney call this "Making Magical Moments." Those daily special instances in their theme parks when a Disney "cast member" notices, for example, that an elderly couple needs assistance taking a photograph or a young family appears totally lost somewhere between Tomorrowland and The Teacups. The cast member then takes a moment out of their normal work routine to personally take charge of that guest-in-need. Disney cast members are required to seek out these moments to make the proverbial Disney magic. It's job one, whether they're a vice president of finance, a street sweeper, or Goofy. To emphasize the importance of those moments, Disney recognizes the achievements of their cast members with "Guest Fanatic Awards," and individuals and organizations in the private sector as "Dreamers and Doers."

Why? Because many corporations—whether they are a fish market, theme park, restaurant, an airline, or even an in-patient health clinic—now understand that in today's marketplace a customer must have a memorable "experience" with their company or product to make an impact. Indeed, questions that marketing gurus ask themselves in countless we-need-an-edge-up-on-the-competition meetings are, "How does the customer's relationship with our business, representative of our business, and our product make the customer feel?" "What's their experience?" Positive emotional reactions to not only the product, but to the entire experience with the company, are paramount.

Let's turn up the heat, and boil that down to you. When it comes down to a one-to-one relationship, Service 101 tells us that if you make a positive impression on a client or customer, that's well, great. But if you care enough to make someone's day, to take a moment to make a moment—if they have a positive emotional experience with you—now, that's fabulous! And memorable. And highly profitable.

Day to day life is much the same, minus the billboards and telemarketing.

However, Service 101 doesn't tell us how to make a genuine positive impression. Or create a genuine positive relationship. Or even how to recognize those golden moments. How do you make it real, every day? Simple. You guessed it—use the tools and spirit of improvisation.

Everyone Loves a Gift

If you pay attention and keep your antennae up, you will notice people present you with "gifts." In improvisation, the term "gifting" is used when someone gives you a gem to work with; your scene partner will make a declaration or tell you information that moves the scene forward. The inexperienced improviser may pass right over the information and take the scene in the direction they have scripted in their head, wasting the gift.

The experienced improviser will use active listening skills and weave the new information, or the "gift," in the scene. The same can be done with customer relationships. People give us gifts all the time. The mother who is struggling with her twins at the grocery store, sighing, closing her eyes to control her temper. She is saying, "Help me! Give me a sucker, something—anything to calm down these kids." The man who buys a car for himself and while shopping tells you about his daughter, who just got her driver's permit, is gifting you with information. He is saying, "I may be looking for another car soon." Each time you receive a gift you are making a moment, moving your relationship forward. (And possibly clinching a new sale.) When you accept gifts you help yourself *and* create a favorable impression with your customers.

As an individual, your effect on others (customers, colleagues) can be long term. However, to make this long-term impression we know that your personal "experience" relationships are really a series of moments. Yes, it all comes down to "making moments."

Okay, what is "making a moment"? Making a moment is the essence of good improvisation scene work. It is first intuitively acknowledging that this moment is an important crossroads in a scene. Saying "yes" to it. Then exploring all the potential in the moment, making a choice, heightening that choice, and letting the chips fall where they may.

Here are some examples of making moments. They can be as small as:

- A wink
- A sincere, unsolicited compliment
- A smile
- Helping a colleague without being asked

Or as large as:

- Sending a thank you bouquet
- Putting a treat and a note in your child's lunch box
- Donating a kidney (just wanted to see if you were still with us)
- Exchanging the usual car mechanic's roast for Starbucks coffee at your weekly meeting
- Giving an on-the-spot coworker massage (if you don't work in litigationville)

A Week's Worth of Moments

Keep your Improvise This! journal, or Palm Pilot if you're electronically inclined, at hand and observe specific life-scene moments in your workplace where "moments could've been made." The list should include moments by a colleague or by you. Briefly describe the moment, and list what the improvisation possibilities are to spontaneously "make a moment." Keep them simple! It could look something like this:

Life Scene: I noticed that Sarah's assistant Marla was never introduced to the clients who passed by her desk.

Possible moment: Sarah could surprise Marla by introducing her to an important client as "Marla the Magnificent—my associate, and the real brains behind the company!"

Life Scene: Sam had just been in an automobile fender-bender, and he's having a tough time getting to the office.

Possible Moment: Tom, who is on Sam's sales team, could print up a couple of coupons that read "Tom's Temporary Taxi Service—good for three free rides to the headquarters and back," and lay them on Sam's desk.

Life Scene: On my way to work, a young woman was selling roses on the highway. I pulled over and bought a dozen.

Possible Moment: And when everyone was out during lunch I could put a rose on the chair of each of my associates, with a note saying: "From a not-so-secret admirer of your incredible work every day! Thanks for everything, Madeline."

True Touching Story

At an airport in New York, the young woman in front of us at the Northwest Skycap check-in encountered a—hmm, how shall we say this?—jerk. He was late for his plane and took it out on this woman. He kicked her bags over with his foot and called *her* an idiot for packing so much! When the self-important Neanderthal walked away she began to cry. Now here's the moment: The skycap shook his head and said, "Every once in a while someone behaves that way. It's sad really, especially when it's directed at someone like you." She was holding her hand over her chest, trying to stop crying, and said, "He just took me by surprise. What did I do?" The skycap, noticing where she had placed her hand, told her that women hold their hand over their hearts to protect it. And went on to tell her that instead of feeling angry and sad, she should use this experience to reflect how lucky she was that she wasn't like that man. He then took her hands, looked her in the eye and said, "It's people like you, kind, caring, people that make me feel the world is truly a good place." For one split second the world stopped. It was like a modern *Little House on the Prairie*. The whole exchange lasted probably two and a half minutes. And it changed that woman's entire day.

(Note to that "one" reader: There is going to be one of you out there who will send us a letter pointing out this was not just "a moment." In reality it was two and a half moments. Don't. Get a life. You know what we mean.)

Moment Mentality

Live life as a series of moments. Look through the eyes of opportunity. Remember the waiter at the restaurant in Florida? Taking a risk and moving Molly's chair not only got a huge laugh, it made a moment—and a memory. When you "throw away the script" and react "in the moment" it makes the scenes of your life sing and your cash register ring.

TIPS ON THE TOPIC

- Smile! Check in with yourself throughout the day to make sure your face is communicating the message you want it to.
- Create positive impressions. Treat each interaction as a new "service scene."
- Make your company a living, breathing, feeling entity.
- Accept gifts by actively listening and act upon the new information.
- Check your company for *Stepford* service mentality.
- Make someone's day. Today.

INDIVIDUAL EXERCISE '10
Make a Week's Worth of Moments

This exercise may leave you feeling like a puppy—awkwardly running around lapping the hand or ankle of anyone in sight you try to please. But remember, making moments can be subtle. By definition a moment is a "brief instant in time." The cumulative effect is what's important. Ready? It's time to take each moment personally.

The Players: "One is the loneliest number . . ." You.

The Object: Take a moment to make a moment three times a day for seven days, at work, play, or anywhere in between.

How To: Commit to put your energy out (not in) and ob-
           serve moment-making opportunities. Immediately
           (without judgment or second-guessing) take the
           leap, and take action with those your gut tells you
           are important. Remember, the action can be small
           and simple! At the end of each day, take simple
           notes in your Improvise This! journal:

           • The moments I identified.
           • The moments I took action. Why. How.
           • The moments I let slip by. Why. How.
           • How did I feel?

The Result: Living "in the moment" during the scenes of your
           life will begin to have concrete, positive payoffs for
           you and those around you.

Throw Away the Script!

AN INSIDE TIP FROM OUTSIDE THE BOX

DARREN OLIVER

Corporate Executive and Improviser

Darren Oliver has worked for several prestigious companies, including the Paris–Las Vegas Resort and Casino. He's currently the vice president of people at Kaiser Permanente Health Plan–Hospitals, California. Darren is married and is the father of three boys; he uses improvisation both at work and at home each and every day. Before this interview we received a call from Darren's assistant, who requested a list of questions for Darren so he could prepare. When we called Darren to go over the questions, he said, "Isn't this about improvisation? Oh, come on. Let's just have some fun."

Q: Darren, how were you first introduced to improvisation?

A: *I'd say it was when I was a facilitator of a career-planning workshop about fifteen years ago. It was a structured course, but I had to rely upon a lot of life experiences to give examples of the lessons I was teaching. When I prepared, I only gave general topics and left details for the actual presentation. If I knew the topic and then improvised, I found I was much more comfortable, genuine, and effective in relating to the audience.*

Q: So, you weren't formally introduced to it?

A: *Well, I never really understood it until I saw a show at Disney World and I was just blown away. I didn't see the connection between what I was doing in training and what they were doing onstage. I thought what they were doing was more pure genius then actual skill. I didn't think I had the capacity to do that. Then I realized that—I do it! (Big hearty laugh)*

Q: Tell us about why you brought improv training to both of the companies you worked for.

A: *In Las Vegas, we found that although people were trained in procedures they didn't know how to make people feel good. Teaching improv skills is the way to go. It liberates people and helps them feel good about their jobs. Basically what we discovered is that when employees feel good, customers feel good. They could be more of themselves. But you can't just teach it, you have to live it. At the Paris–Las Vegas we were trying to teach* joie de vivre. *It's about enjoying food, wine . . . life! I was presenting a training to a large group of people and thought, How do I communicate this? I don't have anything. I could take off my shirt . . . my pants (a bit extreme). I needed to demonstrate a zest for fun. So, I took off my shoes and said, "This feels good. Everybody take off your shoes." No one did it but one guy. I thought, "This is bombing." Interestingly, it became a tradition! You never know how you will develop traditions—and they don't come from manuals. By the way, I'm now the "shoe guy."*

At Kaiser we use improvisation because of our commitment to personalized care. It doesn't get any more personal than health care. If we are really that serious about personalized care, then it's incumbent upon us to know everything there is to know, and do everything there is to do to connect with our members.

Q: So, we see how you use it at work, do you ever use it at home?

A: *Oh yeah! (He laughs) My boys are ten, nine, and five; their interests include the Backstreet Boys and Limp Bizkit. (Sigh) It's hard to connect. So we have fun in other ways; we improvise all the time. We make up stuff together—that's our thing. For instance we may start singing and may even change the words. (Darren begins to sing a song from the movie* Little Nicky, *improvising the words.) It makes us laugh. When you improvise, you share emotions. Here's a great story—not mine—but a great story. Paul Pusateri [former president of Paris–Las Vegas] was taking his kids through the car wash and in the middle of it, he rolled down the windows! The kids loved it; thought it was hysterical . . . his wife didn't feel the same way. I've often thought about doing that, but it would be planned, it just wouldn't be the same.*

Q: It seems car washes are great places to improvise! Last question, is there one pearl of wisdom you would like to share with our readers?

A: *I think people are reluctant to make the connection between improv and business. They think of Robin Williams running around the stage with a brick wall behind him, so it's difficult. It's about taking chances and connecting with people on a deep emotional level.*

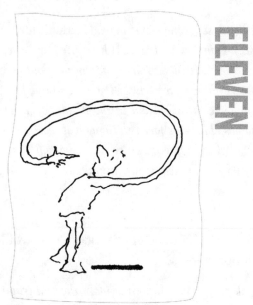

ELEVEN

BLACKOUT!

The End of the Beginning

Calling one's work theatre, treating it accordingly, and developing the capability to influence perceptions through performance separates the magical from the mundane.
—Joseph Pine II and James H. Gilmore, *The Experience Economy*

And . . . Blackout!

The scene is over. The curtain is about to come down on
*Improvise This! How to Think on Your Feet So You Don't Fall on Your
Face.* We assume that you haven't indeed taken a header and
fallen on your face so far in the course of reading this book and
experimenting with its contents—or if you have, you've
dusted yourself and your psyche off, and pressed onward. It's

now time to sit back, relax, and review your experience with improvisation—so far. In this final chapter we're going to help you decompress, debrief, and declare your next small step leading to your next great leap in improvising the scenes of your life—indeed to transform the mundane into the magical in your personal performance.

Let's begin by revisiting this essential point: Improvising (in any situation—a speech, a conversation, in interpersonal communication, in a business relationship) is by nature a first-draft experience. Each of us has many scenes to improvise every day—personal, professional, large and small. Some may be big, splashy Broadway musical scenes that seem to last a lifetime, others are minor dramas that open and close in a moment. And because they are first drafts, how we perform in them is going to be sometimes messy and imperfect. Your performances might range from "Oh my God, I can't believe I actually went with my impulse and challenged my client to a game of wastepaper basketball while we were waiting for the contracts to be printed," to "I nailed it. I was really in the moment when I used 'Yes . . . And!' with my wife, and after two years of her asking, I finally agreed to volunteer for Habitat for Humanity. I had fun, and it felt great helping someone." And everywhere in between.

Here's the key: Laugh at and learn from your successes and failures in this new life skill called improv, and armed with new insight, do it all over again.

THE "GO 'ROUND"

A wonderful method of gaining this insight is a form of analysis that we use in our theatrical improvisation comedy groups and have also adapted for our corporate playshops—a debriefing session called a "Go 'Round." Simply put, in our theatrical groups the actors gather immediately following their performance (while smoking too many cigarettes) and go around the room, person by person, to discuss and dissect the improv show and each actor's contribution. The overriding goal is not only to discover exactly what happened (or what didn't happen) in the performance itself, but also to dissect the process that unfolded on the stage that particular evening. (Not only what they did—equally as important, how they did it.) In our corporate playshops, this go 'round is much the same, with the exception of the details of the "outcomes" or "take-aways" portion of the discussion (and the cigarettes, and sometimes the beer). Now it's time for a personal "go 'round" after reading this book.

Your Personal "Go 'Round"

There are only a few guidelines we will use in any go 'round, including yours. These are designed to keep the analysis objective, supportive, and goal oriented: "What did we (I) do? How did we (I) do it? What can we (I) do to make it better the next time?

- **Be supportive.** Understand that every improviser is at her or his own personal level of development—positive remarks are at least as important and constructive as negative.
- **Be objective.** Offer the gift of observation rather than the slings and arrows of criticism and judgment.
- **Be constructive.** Your comments should take the form of suggestions for improvement.
- **Be honest.** Straightforward observations offered in a positive spirit, even though harsh in content, become wonderful tools for growth and discovery.

- **Be the solution.** As you identify the specific areas you need to improve, it is up to you to take action.

Here we go. Grab a glass of water or wine, a pen or pencil, turn to the final pages of your Improvise This! journal and, using these five pithy points as a format, let's begin to analyze what you've experienced. Here is a sample of what your personal go 'round might look like:

On *Be Supportive:* Give yourself liberal doses of credit for the simple things you've already accomplished by coming this far. It might start as basic as the following:

I give myself credit for:

Trying something new by purchasing this book.

Sticking with it, and reading the whole book.

Attempting all the exercises.

Trying some of the exercises—the ones I felt most comfortable doing.

Taking a moment to make a moment when I:

_____

Each time I actually used one of the improv tools, such as "active listening," like when I:

_____

On *Be Objective:* Put what you've experienced so far into perspective. Quiet that internal voice of self-criticism (let's call him Carl), with a firm "Shut up already!" Now that you have digested the information and concepts in the book and have experimented with an exercise or improvisation tool, ask yourself, What did I observe? How did I feel?

I observed that: It was easy to say "Yes" to more in my life, but much harder to add the ". . . And."

I felt that: I have less fear about improvising each time I finish an exercise.

I observed that: In practicing the "five small steps" in chapter 2, I identified an area of my life I wanted to explore and heighten.

I felt that: I received a lot of resistance when I suggested a creative meeting alternative to my staff. I have two choices: I can either fire them all, or I can improvise other ways to present the same idea.

On *Be Constructive:* For this section, refer back to the chapter on "Yes . . . And!" and your thought sequence. The "Yes" statements may be positive or negative. The "And!" responses are statements of constructive intent:

Yes, I skimmed the book:	And . . . I'll go back and read it cover to cover.
Yes, I want to become more spontaneous:	And . . . I'll start small, but really work on "going with my gut" each day.
Yes, I want to focus new improv skills:	And . . . I'll try that speaker exercise with a friend to get feedback.

On *Be Honest:* Honesty is always dicey, isn't it? Especially when no one else is in the room except you and your face in the mirror. Of course we want you to be honest throughout this go 'round. In this section, complete truthfulness is the tool:

To be honest:

I didn't read the whole book.

The exercises scare me.

I felt more playful than I've felt in a long time when I tried to stay in the moment.

I think this stuff can really work!

On *Be the Solution:* Now that you are near the end of your go 'round and your self-analysis, it's time for action. These final solution statements are "take action declarations" that refer to the challenges you've listed. These are personal commitments to push through your own barriers and become a more consistent, more effective improviser. On one hand, it's important to make the commitments realistic. You may just be in for bitter disappointment if the first item on your list looks like this:

I commit to:

Lose 170 pounds, dump my worthless spouse, find my dream career, and discover love and the cure for Lyme disease all through improvisation techniques—in the next thirty-six hours.

On the other hand, it is equally necessary to make each commitment a challenge to change and to excel in what you now consider your weaknesses. Here we go:

I commit to:

> Read the book a second time.
>
> Complete and repeat every improv exercise.
>
> Have more fun in my life, starting today.
>
> Trust my instincts, and manage my fear of spontaneity in my next life-scene.
>
> Take the next small step to become a better improviser—right now.

Those were the examples. Now, write your own. We'll wait . . .

Finished? Excellent work! You've completed your first personal go 'round. Now, we hear you asking yourself, What in the name of heaven do I do with it now? Here's the answer. Remember, in theatrical improv groups and with corporations we go 'round after every performance or playshop. They're critical to clarity and growth. Use this technique on your own to chart your personal progress as an improviser and map your own goals day to day and week to week.

THE NEXT SMALL STEP: IMPROVISATION AS A TEAM SPORT—TAKE THIS CLASS . . . PLEASE

Okay, here's a good one. "A blind woman, the president of a marketing firm, and an airline pilot walk into an improvisa-

tion class . . ." Sound like a classic barroom joke? It isn't.
Again, it's true. We have taught countless improvisation
classes where the mix of players is at least this wildly varied
and interesting. Risk takers from all walks of life have discovered the childlike joy of getting in tune with the spontaneous
intuitive self that lies beneath the surface of their adult per-
sonas in a group atmosphere. Each individual is motivated
differently: The woman who was sight-impaired had a burn-
ing desire to work on her skills as a storyteller. The president
of the marketing firm was in the midst of a midlife funk and
had merely decided to change his entire career, his long-term
personal relationships, and his way of viewing the world. He
thought that an improv class would give him a jump start. Finally, the airline pilot felt, in his words, "stuck." Not on the
tarmac waiting for the end of gridlock at La Guardia, but
stuck in a personal rut. All three had the courage to sign up
on a whim (making the first choice, taking that first risk), and
before the dust on the stage had settled, stayed for an average
of thirty weeks of classes. Thirty weeks! Why? Because each
was passionate—ready, willing, and able to reach down deep
and rediscover something essential in themselves: their intuitive playful creative spirit. Each also felt the sustaining energy and support that comes from playing within a group of
like-minded improv adventurers.

Sounds exciting, doesn't it? We strongly urge you to consider signing up for an improvisation workshop. The woods
are full of them! Chicago's Second City, the Brave New
Workshop in Minneapolis, the Upright Citizens Brigade in
New York, SAK Theater in Orlando, Paul Sills's Wisconsin
Theater Game Center, and the Groundlings in Los Angeles
(just to name a few) have wonderful schools. Not to mention

(but we will, of course) our own Out-of-the-Blue Improvisation Playshops, which we hold in various locations around the country (www.outofthebluecreative.com).

Our cagey advice: Audit a class or two to find the best instructor. Look for those teachers who are supportive, whose classes reverberate with laughter, and who have their students spend more time on stage doing and discovering than listening to him or her go on about their own acting career.

Sign up and sail off into a potentially life-altering experience. (We've done it, and we've never been the same.)

ANOTHER SMALL STEP—START YOUR OWN
IMPROVISATION GROUP AND PLAY AT WORK

You've guessed it. The ideas and tools you've read about and played with in this book can adapt perfectly to a group setting at work. We've talked a lot about how companies large and small can and do use "Yes . . . And!" and "active listening," for example, every day to great effect. Equally as effective is this wild notion—that you as an individual can spread the word and play at improv where you work.

As we all certainly know by now, corporate cultures are changed not by a flashy new mission statement, a redesigned headquarters building, or the new "Hawaiian shirts every other Wednesday" dress code. Corporate cultures are changed inch by inch and day by day with leadership not only from above, but also from within and from the bottom up. So, what are we suggesting? Nothing less than for you to become the self-inspired improv coach for your organization, no matter where you are on the ladder. Are you ready? Yes, you are, and if you're game, read on. Remember, think big, but start with small steps.

Improvise This! at Work

- Seek out people of like mind and discuss ways of making your workplace improv-friendly.
- Start your day, short midday brain-break, or company event with an improv-based exercise as a warmup or a cooldown.
- At the end of the above meeting (right around the time the attendees are shuffling papers and reaching for their cell phones in unison), suggest an immediate short five-minute creative brainstorm session with a goal to jazz up your next gathering.
- Play! At the next company holiday party or employee appreciation day, cast a group of coworkers to write and perform a comic sketch or song.

YET ANOTHER SMALL STEP—START AN
IMPROVISATION CLUB

We've all heard the expression, "Don't try this at home. Leave it to the professionals." It doesn't apply to improvisation. Another wonderful opportunity to share in the pleasure and challenges of this experience is to form an improvisation club with friends or in your community. Here's how:

- Find a community space. (A school classroom or home recreation room will do nicely.)
- Use this book as your workbook.
- Play the games. Meet to discuss how the drills and exercises within have worked for each. Do them in front of the group.
- Share insights with one another on what positive personal change has occurred by practicing the ideals and using the tools of improvisation. (Support, support, support.)

By taking the first step to use improvisation techniques at work or with a group of friends, you will encourage others to join in on the fun and throw away the script of their routine. Who knows? You just might coach them to break a few barriers along the way and create a more spontaneous, energized work or group environment. And to help you make the leap, read on. Since you've played the games so well, we've provided you with "Group Games People Play for Fun and Profit" in the Epilogue as our parting gift to you.

FINAL, WE REALLY MEAN IT, FINAL TIPS ON THE TOPIC OF HOW TO "IMPROVISE THIS!"

- Lather, Rinse, and Repeat. Take a cleansing breath or two, and read the book again. Use a pen or highlighter (any color, we don't care) and view it this time through as a workbook. Go back and repeat the exercises. Each tool and exercise is critical to building your foundation.
- Take what you do seriously, and take yourself lightly. The spirit of fun is essential to your growth as an improviser. Challenge yourself to discover enjoyment every day, as you live in the moment.
- In practice, remember that improvisation is not a "head game" where you spin your wit-wheels to think up a just-right joke or a snappy comeback. It's really a "heart game." You're learning an infinitely more fulfilling skill; you're learning to actively listen to the deeper creative voice in you that knows exactly what to do in any life scene.
- Commit. Commit. Commit!

Above all, "Life is improvisation." We don't pretend to have all the answers to triple sales in your department, turn a rabid customer into your lapdog, or to solve the crisis in the Middle East. (Although a little "Yes . . . And!" and "give and take" between the leader/combatants at the peace talk marathons might just be the ticket.) We do know firsthand, however, that living the ideals and using the tools of improv can be life changing if you want it to be, whatever the moment, whatever the scene.

Whether it's as earth-shatteringly important as managing a merger meeting or as insignificant as making a seat-of-your-pants wedding toast—make the spontaneous choice to take a chance and enjoy the ride.

The challenge that we issued in chapter 2 bears repeating: Never fear. Or, never let fear get the best of you. Taking the risk to say "Yes" to yourself and to those around you is to laugh at the unknown and to embrace it for what it is—an opportunity to shine, to discover a new way to approach your business or personal relationships, to make it up as you go along. Hey— to improvise!

It's up to you. And when you're in doubt, we believe that this time you won't pull back. We know that this time, you'll play your scenes for all they're worth. We're sure that this time, you'll Improvise This!

You miss 100 percent of the shots you never take.

—Wayne Gretzky

EPILOGUE

Group Games People Play for Fun and Profit

Are you still here?

We think that's great! As promised, here is a sampling of improvisation games you can easily play in a group setting. Before you begin, we suggest you go back to chapter 1 and review with your group how the stage was set for the individual games: "The Experience," "The Atmosphere," the concept of "Lather, Rinse, Repeat," and "The Result."

Now that you're all on the same page and all on the same path, relax, have fun, and Improvise These.

GROUP GAME 1—WARMING UP
Zip! Zap! Zop!

The Players: Three to thirteen.

The Object: Passing positive energy out to the group. Remember "energy out" versus "energy in." Teamwork. Eye contact. Focus. Concentration.

How To: Form a circle. The first player slaps his or her hands together and points at another player. Making eye contact, the first player shouts, "Zip!" (He or she has passed the "energy" of the *Zip!*)

     The receiving player then repeats the hand motion, makes that important eye contact with another random player, and shouts, "Zap!" That player repeats the same with "Zop!"

     Now—here's where the fun comes in: The next player goes back to Zip! And so on. Zip, Zap, Zop.

     Now pick up the pace.

     The focus should be on everyone following each Zip, Zap, Zop whether it comes to him or not.

     Repeat many times randomly around the circle.

The Result: At first, strange looks from the participants. They'll wonder if you're psychotic. Or a preschool teacher. Then they'll get into the flow of energy and refuse to quit. The end result of this warm-up game is a heightened sense of play and in-the-moment individual focus—outward to the group.

GROUP GAME 2 — "YES . . . AND!"
Everybody Go!

The Players: Three to three hundred.

The Object: Support your fellow players. Be loud. Be crazy. Be physical. Don't think—do!

How To: Get in a circle. The first player shouts "Everybody go . . ." and then he or she makes a huge full-bodied physical movement and a big gut-wrenching sound to go with it. (It shouldn't be literal!)

Following this foolishness, everyone in the circle pumps their arms outward and exclaims, "Yes!"

All the players then immediately repeat the movement and sound of the first player—with gusto and commitment. Go around the circle with everyone taking a turn.

The Result: Results, results. Come on! It's a process, not a product. Unclench your jaw right now.

(Oh, all right.) The result: This is a wonderful team-building, team-trust game. If everyone commits to the foolishness, a barrier of self-consciousness is broken. If everyone does it, no one looks like an idiot!

GROUP GAME 3—ACTIVE LISTENING
Simultaneous Talk—Or *Enough About You, What About Me?*

The Players: You, the person that's talking at you, and a facilitator/timekeeper.

The Object: To actively listen (mind and body) to another player's improvised story and retain their literal and emotional content, while simultaneously improvising a story of your own.

How To: Sit facing your fellow player. The facilitator chooses two simple unrelated story topics and gives one to each player. For instance, they might be "cookie" and "wristwatch." When the timekeeper says "Begin," each player, making eye contact with the other, begins to tell an improvised story based on his or her individual topic.

The players must listen *and* improvise simultaneously. After two minutes, the timekeeper announces, "Time."

One of the players then attempts to repeat the other player's story ("cookie") back to him or her word for word. When he or she has repeated the story as much as he or she is able, the other player then repeats the other's story ("wristwatch").

Discuss the results.

The timekeeper then takes the place of one of the players, who assumes the role of timekeeper. The exercise is repeated until all have experienced it at least twice or they are reduced to tears of frustration—whichever comes first.

Hints:
1. Remember eye contact. This keeps your focus on the other player.

2. Descriptive or evocative words and phrases tend to be remembered more easily. Why? Because they paint an image in the listener's mind or cause an emotional response.

3. Don't try too hard to concentrate. Relax and allow your improvised story to simply flow out of you. At the same time, allow your fellow player's story to flow into you.

The Result:
A heightened sense of how our minds race even as we think we're actively listening to another fellow human being, and how little we really do retain. Also, an increased awareness of what information and emotional content we are more likely to retain while listening.

GROUP GAME 4 — "YES . . . AND!" —
BRAINSTORMING AND TEAMWORK
Ad Campaign

The Players: Three to thirteen.

The Object: A five-minute no-holds-barred improvised ad campaign for a fictitious new product. The focus of this exercise is to create a) a new "product," b) the many and varied "uses" for that product, and c) a marketing campaign and a slogan.

How To: Form a circle. Choose an imaginary household object. Imagine that object on a pedestal in the middle of the circle. Let's use "a pencil." The group begins by chanting "pencil—pencil—pencil." Using "give and take" (not stepping on each other's ideas) and "Yes . . . And!"

Using this agreement and support, the players begin free-associating and combining each other's thoughts on the object "pencil."

The Product: As each thought is expressed, the next player who feels the impulse to contribute says "Yes . . . And!" and adds his idea to the pot. Then the next player and the next. Soon the pencil has become a product with new characteristics.

The Uses: Begin the same process and "Yes . . . And!" the uses for the new and improvisationally improved "pencil."

The Marketing: Now that the players know what the pencil looks and feels like and what its uses are, it's time to begin the group brainstorm of the marketing campaign and slogan. The players can sing, dance, rhyme, and chant their way to how to market their product—the "Ultimate Pencil for the New Millennium!"

Hints:

1. Give and Take. Remember it. Some of the more assertive players may attempt to take control. Allow everyone to assert his or her point of view.

2. "Yes . . . And!" Acknowledge and build on each idea. The ideas can be transformed by another player, but not denied.

The Result: By saying "Yes!" to your fellow player's ideas, "And" combining his ideas with your own, players experience a judgment-free brainstorm session where each player's contributions are valued and integrated into the final product.

GROUP GAME 5 — LISTENING, TRUST, TEAMWORK
Voice-Activated Supercomputer

The Players: Three to six. A leader and an audience of peers.

The Object: The team forms a human "supercomputer" and becomes one brain. By linking one word at a time into coherent sentences or concepts, the voice-activated supercomputer answers any and all questions posed to it by the audience.

How To: This game is semi–touchy-feely. You actually must be in close physical proximity with other human beings. (What a concept.)

Line up hip to hip. Each player puts an arm around the waist of the player next to him or her.

A question is posed to the computer. Start simple with something like "Computer, what is the weather going to be like tomorrow?"

The line of players, now the computer, begins to answer—each player in turns says one word at a time to form the answer.

The answer travels right down the line, and then back to the first person. Then down the line again, until the leader feels that the answer is perfect— or perfectly ridiculous.

Repeat until your collective brain is spinning.

Change the team around. Take turns being the leader.

Hints: 1. Have the computer repeat the question one word at a time as they attempt to answer the question.

2. The faster the computer answers the better.

3. Coach the players: Don't try to come up with the whole answer. You're just responsible for one word! Trust your fellow players. Keep the pace up!

The Result: Trust, support, and learning the idea of "giving up to the group," which is sometimes very difficult for hard-pressing future CEOs. As you repeat this exercise and get comfortable with it, you'll find that many of the collective answers become more coherent. Or, if not coherent, screamingly obtuse and nonsensical—which is okay! The players will begin to loosen up and trust the whole team.